Photo by Geo. Bell. Milwaukee, Wis.　　　Courtesy of Woodley Studio, Madison, Wis.

THE DANCE

AND

ITS PLACE IN EDUCATION

*With Suggestions and Bibliography
for the Teacher of the Dance*

BY

MARGARET NEWELL H'DOUBLER, M. A.

ASSOCIATE PROFESSOR IN
THE DEPARTMENT OF PHYSICAL EDUCATION
UNIVERSITY OF WISCONSIN

NEW YORK
HARCOURT, BRACE AND COMPANY

DEDICATED
TO
THE STUDENTS OF THE DANCE
AT
THE UNIVERSITY OF WISCONSIN

" 'Tis to create and in creating live
A being more intense, that we endow with form
Our fancy, gaining as we give
The life we image."

Preface

After the work of developing a type of dancing that should be at once educational and creative had been carried on for several years, the need for some written formulation of the work both as to its aim and its procedure became apparent. An earlier book, "A Manual of Dancing," served for a time until the exhaustion of that edition gave the opportunity to meet the need for a newer and fuller discussion. This book is not offered as a complete treatment of the subject in all its phases. It would be folly to attempt to give in one volume all that is known about the philosophy, history, and science of the dance. But, because the procedure of instruction has been so definitely influenced by conclusions formed from the study of these essential fields, it will be necessary to state the facts which have been accepted, and which are to be considered as points of departure in the further development of this discussion. In all this the writer makes no pretense to an original piece of work. What is offered is only a fresh and different application of long established and well known facts. It was in the general study of the philosophy and science of art that the spirit of the dance was revealed, and it is in this understanding of its true spirit that an attempt has been made to revive the dance.

While the type of dancing discussed in these pages has been used successfully with all ages from elementary school to university and even beyond, and while the general principles are the same for all students, regardless of age, this discussion pays particular attention to the needs and possibilities of older students. Again, this book affords an introduction to the principles and possibilities of the dance that it is hoped may be helpful and interesting to the general reader, but its main interest and appeal lies within the field of education. And while it affords a manual for the student, it is addressed primarily to the teacher. Therefore, if it can serve as a help and a stimulus to the better teaching of the dance in our schools and colleges, it will have fulfilled its purpose.

Inspiration and assistance have been gained from so many sources that it is impossible to make complete and adequate acknowledgment of indebtedness to individuals or to the works of others. Special mention should be made, however, of the inspiration received from the work of Alys E. Bentley. Grateful acknowledgment is also made to all those students and friends who have aided in the preparation of this manuscript, and to those students whose patient coöperation in the application of principles which were not yet fully established made this book in its present and final form possible.

M. N. H'D.

Contents

Contents

Foreword

Some systematic physical recreation, some education
of the body, has come to be a requirement in practically
all colleges where women are being educated. In univer-
sality this requirement stands along with the requirement that each college student shall learn some power to
express herself in her mother tongue, and that she shall
know at least a little of the literature in which her race
has set down a record of its heart's desires. Like the
power to use the mother tongue and the knowledge of
what her ancestors have held to be good and beautiful
in life, this physical education is meant to give the college woman a habit that will carry beyond her campus
days, a resource for happy living. Many thoughtful
observers of the physical education requirement in the
college curriculum would accept as a test of its success
the extent to which the exercise required in college remains the recreation of later years.

For this reason colleges have substituted physical activities of many kinds for the more fixed and precise
drill which older college women remember. So varied
are these that it seems reasonable to hope that every
student will find something which she does well enough
to give her keen immediate pleasure, so that she will
keep a little time for physical play even when life crowds
her hours with other things. College departments of
physical education are accordingly always seeking for activities least likely to be interrupted when the college

woman finds herself in a tiny village, with no swimming-pool or bathing beach, no lake or river for her canoe, no bowling alley, not even a frosty winter to spread snow for her skiis or snowshoes or toboggan. Furthermore, college realizes that if possible the college woman needs a physical recreation that does not depend upon finding a number of others skilled and ardent in the same activity, for in her remote village the college hockey or tennis champion may fail to find the playmates necessary to give her a tingling, exhilarating hour.

Students at the University of Wisconsin have now for seven years been fortunate in having the privilege of such an activity in Professor Margaret H'Doubler's classes in interpretative dancing.

This work I saw first not in any laboriously rehearsed public program, but in an ordinary class hour. It was in the dark era when the natural delight in rhythmic motion had small chance of gratification. Fashion had reduced ordinary social dancing to a graceless lurching or tottering or lunging about to the accompaniment of strident, unmelodious sounds, beating a barbaric reiteration of a crass or meaningless phrase. The only other type of dancing was of an elaborate pattern requiring practically professional aptitude and skill. Consequently it was surprising and delightful to find that Miss H'Doubler's modest and cordial invitation to "come up and see a class at work" had introduced me to a group of college girls who were dancing with great joy what excellent music meant to each of them. Music at that dreary period was exiled from social dances, but here students were entering into intimate and real possession of some of the most beautiful things humanity has achieved.

Physical education was quietly putting these young women into vital relationship with an element of our civilization that is of the spirit as well as of the senses. Body was being made capable in this education of expressing what the mind heard and felt. Body and soul were well at home together in that hour of dancing; there was no topsy-turvy confusion as to which was master and which was joyously responsive servant. There was here no unenlightened paganism bidding the mind to crouch or sleep and inviting the physical to make itself all-sufficient and dominant. Life in that dancing class had a happy and excellent unity. The delight of responsive nerves and muscles blended with the delight in good music.

There is little doubt that some students were enjoying music of a higher quality than they had been in the habit of liking. No arbiter of taste, telling them that they ought to enjoy it, could have had the effect which came naturally from hearing it over and over and receiving it more intensely because of the bodily expression of its rhythm.

Similarly, through the dramatic element of the dancing, the dancers were brought into touch with some of the most charming and most significant things which the race has embodied in literature and in plastic or pictorial art. So this dancing was not a glorification of the body for its own sake: it linked the joy of physical activity with the pleasure of the mind in things approved as charming and worthy.

In another respect, too, this dancing was delightful (the impression of that first day has been borne out by six years of observing the work): the dancers were not exploiting themselves; they were not vying with each other. There was no competition, no grasping self-assertion, no disappointment. What one got took nothing from the others. Each expressed as adequately as she could in her own way what the music and the dramatic situation meant to her. There were no points, no score; no winning, no losing. The moments had a quality that were self-sufficient; they had no need to be summed up or appraised.

It was not merely the absence of individual self-striving; it was the positive realization that the group was the medium of expression rather than the single person. One of the most gifted dancers has always preferred to be one of a group rather than to dance alone. So this kind of dancing is an activity that expresses and fosters a generous social spirit. One might truly say that a deeper rhythm than that of any music is thus found and satisfied in these class hours. To be intent and not tense, to feel one's own life richly and profoundly and at the same time to feel the joy of comradeship—that is what this dancing of college girls at the University of Wisconsin has seemed to be to one who looked on.

It is therefore with warm interest that I have seen this beautiful educational activity pass to other communities, and that I see it now go to the still wider circle which this book may reach.

F. LOUISE NARDIN,
Dean of Women.

Madison, Wisconsin,
　　September 30, 1924.

THE DANCE

AND

ITS PLACE IN EDUCATION

Chapter I

THE PROBLEM

Before undertaking the more logical development of our discussion, it may be of value to set down those observations and reflections which have led the writer to conceive of the dance as an educational force, and which will establish the line of thought upon which the whole discussion is based.

The dance has suffered too long from the common use made of it as a means of recreation and amusement. Modern civilization has not usually considered it either worthy of serious effort or intellectually profitable. Only recently has progressive education recognized the value of physical education. The dance has shared in this recognition, but only as a part of physical education. Even there it finds but a small place, and is forced to assume many guises to hold its place. But as more students with a real scholarly interest enter the field of physical education, they are realizing that its program has too long ignored the relation between body and soul as expressed in regulated rhythm—not the rhythm that is experienced when mass drill is regulated by music, nor the rhythm of the body in vigorous muscular activity,

The figure drawings used in this book are copyrighted by Miss Bernice Oehler. They were developed from quick action sketches of dancers in class work.

3

nor the rhythm of group marching, but the rhythm that is felt when the rhythm of bodily activity is associated with the deeper and finer currents of man's emotional nature.

The very nature of the modern world makes it imperative that such provision be made. Our age is one of industrialism and materialism. The routine of the office and the "piece-jobs" of the factory rob the worker of any opportunity to identify himself with his work. They do not afford him any opportunity for appreciating or creating beauty of form either physical or spiritual. It is no wonder that he and his fellows flock to the dance halls and movies to satisfy their need for self-expression and a wider experience. Nor is the time much more favorable to the more cultivated and intellectual. When we reflect on the opportunity that primitive man even in his convention-bound world had for self-education and the enlarging of his imagination by free and impulsive expression, we can appreciate one of the defects of our so-called culture. With the progress of civilization, the impulse to give vent to our feelings has been brought too rigidly under the domain of our reason. The world in which we live affords little opportunity for the individual to grow by the exercise of his creative impulses. He is reduced to mere imitation. It is true that we are no longer in the primitive stage of culture, but when we realize the important rôle that self-expressive activities have played in the evolution of the race, we can more justly appreciate the necessity of finding a place for them in our lives to-day. For man cannot live fully on his intellect alone; the artist lying dormant in him must be allowed to develop. Psychology teaches us that education proper does not begin until the individual has begun to try to realize his ideals in the world without. In other words, it recognizes the importance of creative activity in the development of the mind. Without the opportunity to body forth the aspirations of the self, we may never realize with what powers we are endowed. And without some provision for our sense of beauty we are more than likely to continue that failure to appreciate the world we live in, which for all our material triumphs leaves the life of our age so joyless for vast numbers of men.

Here our education has not succeeded in helping our people to that art spirit which they so much want. The fault is mainly with our conceptions of educational values. Too often we have not given a place to the appreciation and love of beauty in a scheme of education meant to prepare one for the serious business of living. With far too many people, education has been looked upon as a means of bettering one's economic condition, and not as a way of making a more adequate man of oneself. It seems almost as if the aim were to be a success in business, instead of a successful human being.

But now our advances in education are intensifying the very needs that education has long disregarded. We are paying more attention to the individual than we have paid for a long time; we are encouraging him to discover and to express himself. We are encouraging him to go out for what he wants. And yet too often we fail to give him adequate acquaintance with the various planes of desirable things that he may learn to discriminate and to elect the higher rather than the lower in entertainment and recreation as well as in the graver undertakings of life. And where our education fails to make such provision, it is falling short as education. For the aim of education, as Henmon has aptly defined it, is "To bring an individual from where he is to where he ought to be." Or to say the same thing with more particular regard to art, the problem is how to keep alive the creative impulse in the child and help carry it over into the realities of adult life with heightened power and more enlightened purpose.

The teacher of any subject who earnestly approaches his task from such a general point of view must feel a deep sense of responsibility and at the same time a sense of great opportunity to serve mankind, and help men to find meaning in life and joy in living it. But, to do this, we as teachers should have some realization of what is for the good of the race in general, and at the same time some understanding of the fundamental principles that serve to realize those racial values in the individual. Man, and all that he does, are the result of the workings of natural laws which were active long before the knowledge was discovered to explain them back to us. It is for this reason that the contributions made to modern education by educational psychology are so valuable. Not only does the study of individual differences, for instance, make clear why we are different, and what the consequences of our differences are, but it also reveals that underneath these differences we are all fundamentally alike. We all have at heart the same feelings and emotions, no matter how different their development into living forces may be because of the influence of education. Consequently, as teachers of the dance, we should question ourselves upon the relation of our art to the basic qualities of human nature. We should ask ourselves such questions as these: Just what do we mean by the dance? Why do we dance? What are the ultimate values and justifications of the dance? Further, what purpose does it serve, what function has it performed in the evolution of society that it has not perished? What is the nature of this urge for self-expression in movement? Finally, what are the educational values of the dance? What does it contribute to the refinement of the student and the cultivation of his artistic life? Such a search into the real nature of the dance will yield us our philosophy of dancing, a philosophy based on a fundamental belief in the æsthetic capacities of man and the real worth of his expressing himself through creative activity, if only he will express the best that is in him. And from this philosophy must be formed a theory that will be at once an expression of the aims for which the dance should work, and a formulation of the fundamental principles underlying it. An example of such a principle is our insistence that the dance be an adequate means of self expression, so that when movement of mind, soul, and body are coördinated, rhythmical, beautiful and expressive movements may result. In order to work toward this end, our theory must be built on a mastery of the structure and the natural movements of the body, and a knowledge of the principles of æsthetics, and a thorough understanding of the psychology of the emotions. This carries us over into what is the science of the dance, the systematized knowledge of cause and effect, which tells us how to adjust our efforts to attain the desired ends. Here, we must distinguish between the art of dancing and dancing as an art. The first, the art of dancing, is the skill which performs the acts directed by science.

Science, to repeat, is systematized knowledge, so art in this sense means knowledge made efficient by skill. It does not go beyond skillful performance. But by dancing as an art, we mean something more,—dancing as an adequate and harmonious means of expressing our emotional life. This second meaning takes us back to our philosophy and brings us once more to the realization that dancing must be genuinely expressive of the inner man if it is to rank with the other fine arts.

To summarize—our problem in teaching is this: First, we must have well defined aims which are in accord with the general aims of education. Second, we must know the individual needs and capacities of our students. Third, we must be masters of our subject matter; and fourth, we must have some scheme or plan for adapting the subject matter to the group so that we may realize our purposes. If then we wish to guide wisely the development of students, we must understand the nature of intelligence, and the psychology of learning. It is only in the light of these considerations that we can wisely choose our material, and devise our method of teaching. In the last analysis it is the development of human nature, of personalities, that is the important consideration, not the subject itself. That is only a means. Our real purpose is to teach boys and girls and men and women by means of the dance; to teach them a philosophy of life that finds its practical application in the dance.

Chapter II

THE DANCE — ITS ESSENTIAL NATURE DEFINED IN
TERMS OF ITS DEVELOPMENT

The story of art is the story of mankind. It covers the whole sweep of human life, changing through the ages as man has changed, varying with his religion, his philosophy and his social relations. When man appeared in this world, he came with no fund of intellectual knowledge or experience behind him. He was forced to rely upon his instincts and what brain he had to bring about an adjustment with the world in which he found himself. Gradually, thanks to the powers of his own nature and the forces of his environment, he developed into a feeling, willing, thinking self. In this slow progress of civilization, art, an activity of man's own creation, has always been a helpful influence. Every age has had its art. This very fact is evidence of its value to man. If it were not of real consequence to the maintenance of society, it would have disappeared by the very laws of natural selection.

When we remember how undeveloped primitive man's mind was, and how rigorous were the conditions in which he lived, we can appreciate that what forms of expression he had were of necessity very close to his life needs, and that these forms must have been crude and utilitarian in their nature.

9

With the savage, expressive acts could have been none other than random, impulsive movements that afforded a quite unconscious outlet to his passing feelings. Gradually they were modified by his growing realization of the effect of his own actions until they finally became consciously and intentionally expressive. It was when thus modified that early man's expressive activities became art. Unfortunately art is thought of by many people only in terms of its highest manifestations as something that exists only in masterpieces in galleries. By the same logic artists have come to be considered as a special class who practice art professionally. Such connotations have made not only the creation of art seem remote from common life but also its appreciation. This is unfortunate and untrue, for as Henri truly says, "Art when really understood is the province of every human being. It is simply a question of doing anything well. It is not an outside, extra thing. When the artist is alive in any person, whatever his kind of work may be, he becomes an inventive, searching, daring, self-expressive creature. He becomes interesting to other people. The world would stagnate without him, and the world would be beautiful with him; for he is interesting to himself and he is interesting to others. He does not have to be a painter or a sculptor to be an artist. He can work in any medium. He simply has to find the gain in the work itself, not outside of it. Museums of art will not make a country an art country. But where there is the art spirit, there will be precious works to fill museums."

Many are the theories that have been propounded to explain art, but whatever definition one accepts, art remains ever the expression of the world's soul. It takes deep root in man's experience. It is an answer to his instinctive craving for expression. The great artist is he who in his individual emotions and experiences reflects the emotions and experiences of all mankind, and so by sympathy and knowledge penetrates more deeply into the hearts and lives of his fellow men. He must be able to experience the hopes and fears, the joys and sorrows, and the aspirations of the world individually and collectively. So art may be defined in its result as the adequate translation of emotional experience into some external form. It is the expression of the feeling within by means of line, or color, or sound, or movement so that others may share the feeling.

No matter how diverse the forms of art, they all take root in man's nature and needs. It cannot be explained, as Hirn so convincingly points out, by play-impulse, or the impulse to attract, or the impulse to imitate, although all of these purposes no doubt have a direct influence on the development of the various forms. Rather, as Hirn goes on to say:

"The impelling force in art-creation is to be explained by the psychology of feeling. Every high strung emotional state, which has not found its appropriate expression, causes movement by which we instinctively try to get rid of the feeling of restraint. . . . Yet art production would never have reached so high a development if it had served only as a sedative for human feelings. Art supplies man with the means of intensifying feelings connected with all the varied activities of the soul, and also bestows an inward calm in which all strong emotions find relief. The world has been measured with man as a standard and objects have been trained into the language of mental experiences. Impressions have gained thereby not only in emotional tone but also in intellectual comprehensibility. So irreconcilable is the conflict between the emotional excitation and the intellectual activity that the latter, when it expressly serves the purpose of emotional enhancement, must neutralize the excess of feelings."

This instinct to express all feeling in order to continue pleasurable states of feeling, and to obtain relief from that which is not pleasurable, has its basis in the physiological phenomena of all life. We see it manifested in the movement of the lowest form of life we know, the amoeba, in its going out toward stimuli which are pleasant and its withdrawal from those stimuli that are unpleasant. And so throughout our complex life our habits depend on this physiological fact of reacting to pleasant and unpleasant stimuli. All movement, no matter how complex, is essentially built up on this instinctive expansion and contraction. It is also instinctive to try to give external reality to our feelings in such a way as to bring others to partake of the same emotional experience. This transmission of feeling to others and the response of other people to one's own emotion really enhances the original emotional state of the creator—which is another source of pleasure in artistic effort. It was this desire to perpetuate his thoughts and feelings that led man in the first place to discover a way of translating them through whatever medium he had at hand and as well as he could within the limits of his powers of execution. It is this craving to have others feel as we do, to experience the enrichment of their response to our feeling that has led to artistic production. Man feels the need, but it is the artist in him that discovers the way of satisfying it; imagination fashions the means out of the background of experience. In art, as in everything else, "necessity is the mother of invention." In other words, back of all the various manifestations of art, and in all its stages from that in which it was merely a crude spontaneous reflex of strong feeling, to those forms that express man's highest emotional life, the one fundamental impulse is the same—the craving for self-expression.

Of course not everyone can be an artist in the narrow sense of the word. But if we recognize that it is the nature of the original impulse that leads to creative activity, and the emotional value of its expression which distinguishes any activity as art, then we shall see that anyone who approaches his work in a creative spirit and makes it the expression of his own vision of life is an artist. As Hirn says, "From the point of view of artistic perfection, there is all the world between the youthful verses of Goethe and the doggerel of a common schoolboy. But, psychologically the schoolboy's doggerel may be the result of as strong a craving for poetic expression as any of the world's greatest poems. . . . If the notion of art is conceived in its most general sense, every normal man, at some time of his life at least, is an artist, in aspiration, if not in capacity." Noyes carries the same thought a step farther—"The impulse to expression is common to all, the difference is one of degree. And the message of art is for all, according as they are attuned to the response. Art is creation. For the artist it is creation by expression; for the appreciator it is creation by evocation. These two principles complete the cycle; abstractly and briefly they are the whole story of art. To be responsive to the needs of life and its emotional appeal is the just condition of artistic creation. By new combinations of material elements to bring emotion to expression in concrete harmonious forms, themselves charged with emotion and communicating it—is to fashion a work of art. To feel in material whether in the forms of nature or in the works of art, a meaning for the spirit, is the condition of appreciation."

In other words, man needs to realize his dream of life in some form outside of himself. This necessity is one of the most important keys to his history. We may observe its working in all that he does, in speech, in dress, in manner, in fact in all his inventions. As he reached higher planes of thought, this desire for expression demanded, of course, more appropriate means. So there gradually evolved what are termed the fine arts—dance, music, poetry, drama, architecture, painting, sculpture. These differ in form, but they all have a common source in the fundamental human need of setting forth its inner life in an external form. In speaking of art we must not let the particular kind of activity that produces artistic results become divorced from those everyday, common actions and experiences. The difference is only one of degree. From the disappointments, joys and sorrows of actual ordinary life, we build a world of meanings, we think of things as we wish they might be, we idealize. Art affords us the opportunity of experiencing, of actually living these dreams. Art is life as we would have it.

In these ways, all the arts are really one. But at the same time, each art has its own peculiar province, its own purposes and its own ways. So with the dance.

Psychology teaches us that all mental activity (both

thought and feeling) tends to express itself in muscular and glandular activity. Every thought or impression from the external world entering consciousness by way of the senses must find itself an outlet. In all early life (whether it be that of the primitive man or the young child) the natural discharge is over the motor nerve paths to the muscles. Thus it is that we find mere random movements the most immediate expression of simple feeling. But these movements that are merely a reflex accompaniment of feeling cannot yet be called the dance. For the same reason we cannot call the joyous running and leaping against the wind, art; but if we take the leaps and runs and the various reactions to the "feel" of the wind and mold them to the conventions of line, balance and decorum, we shall have art. It is this systematizing according to the laws of the medium that separates art from accident and nature. It is only when these random, yet expressive movements, are subjected to the harmonizing influence of rhythm, or time sequence, that the dance proper comes into being. The delight of vigorous movements that are expressive of joy in living, and of exuberance of energy, is very great, but when rhythm comes in to systematize these chaotic feelings so that there is harmony of motion,—the pleasure of motion may become ecstasy.

But what is rhythm? What is the fundamental fact common to all rhythm that enables us to speak not only of rhythm in the dance but of rhythm in music, rhythm in nature.

Categorically speaking, rhythm is action and rest—control and release; it is measured motion—a periodic repetition. Its presence is manifest in all life even though its ways are devious. It regulates all our organic bodily processes. It serves to facilitate muscular effort alike in the individual and the group; it is capable of emotional enhancement and of symbolic expression; it has the power of moving armies in unison, and of binding all manner of men together in song and dance. It can be explained only in terms of our own being. It is an attribute of man's nature. His whole physiological and psychological functionings obey the laws of rhythm, and out of this involuntary obedience has come the highly conscious appreciation of form. No matter how involved the particular manifestation to which the term is applied, the phenomenon of rhythm harks back to the organization of our nervous system—the thinking, feeling, knowing side of us, which we have observed is so connected with muscles and sense organs, that all sensory stimuli arouse motor reactions. Even where the motor response may be inhibited so far as external results are concerned, the tendency still persists. And further, according to the James-Lange theory, the emotions are the return wave of the reflex muscular and organic changes that accompany the perception of an exciting fact, it being the "feel" of these changes that constitutes the emotion. If we accept this theory, our perception of rhythm, which is an "exciting fact" or stimulus, must depend upon sensations from our muscles. As a matter of fact, rhythm pervades our entire being, regulating our body from the smallest part to the whole. The native persistency of rhythm becomes apparent when we attempt unrhythmic movements. There is a constant tendency to lapse into rhythmic action in spite of great concentration of effort to maintain irregular groupings. Such a process proves very fatiguing. Periodic repetition leads to automaticity; movements that are rhythmically executed gain in ease and grace. In this understanding of the nature of stimulus and response, can be found the explanation of how it is that pure rhythm can convey thought and feeling. The rhythm that exists in any object that is created by man, of necessity is physiologically sensed before it is embodied in the object of its fashioning; this in turn is re-experienced by the observer in its original, rhythmical terms, on the principle that like stimulus produces like response. So we owe it to rhythm that we are able to feel as the composer of any work must have felt. Everyone is also familiar with the part rhythm plays in the recalling of a forgotten tune. Often if the tune can be tapped out, the melody will come to mind. Again, the emotional power of rhythm can be easily shown by the tapping out a series of sounds with due regard to elements of stress and pause and speed, and it will be readily seen that pure rhythmic form is an aid to arousing an emotional state. Because of this stimulating, yet regulating power, rhythm may be considered the foundation of all art.

There is nothing mechanical, however, in the working of rhythm. Although a group may share the same mood aroused by (for convenience, we will say) a selection of music, yet, if each member of the group were asked of what did it remind him, there would probably be as many different interpretations as persons asked, for our feelings are attached to past experience, and each observer can only create out of what he has already actually experienced, or imagined—according to the laws of mental association.

It is for this reason that the real pleasure and value of the objects of art lie not so much in the actual object perceived as in the associations they recall. It is this which gives art its power to stir the imagination, the source of its greatest influence. It is this power to draw upon the emotional stores of the past that gives art its great potency as a civilizing force. Strong feeling seeks stimulation for its relief, but when rhythm comes to its service, the turbulent emotional state is harmonized and tranquilized. The rebellious energies are transformed into a larger understanding and harmony. With primitive man, when rhythm was the only outlet for feeling, there was no other artistic escape for this energy but the movement of the dance. He had to express himself. Music or poetry or drawing were still unknown to him. There was no other medium but his own body through which he might give vent to his feelings. So he danced.

Time will not be given here to a complete historical analysis of the dance in all its forms, or to an encyclopedia of the various dances. Although such a study is closely related to our subject, it is not necessarily a part of it. With so many histories of the dance available it is unnecessary. It is more pertinent for us to draw the necessary general conclusions from such data as are applicable to the whole subject of the dance, and to follow the path the dance has taken in its evolution from the cruder to the more artistic forms, noting as we go its most characteristic technical and social elements.

First of all, the dance is not to be considered peculiar to any one race or nationality. It is inborn, a heritage common to all mankind. It has existed in as many forms

as there are ways of the heart to feel, and these forms have
further varied with the beliefs, customs, and even dress
of the dancers. Every age has had its dance. With
savage man the dance afforded, as we have seen, the one
artistic outlet for his energies, and the one always available medium for the satisfaction of his inborn sense of
rhythm. The earliest savage dances seem to have been
individual dances, consisting of more or less random movements. Later in his development man acquired a group,
and came to feel himself one of a larger unit, which was
both restraining and stimulating to his activities. His
individual desires gave way to the group customs. He
still danced his same love, fear and anger, but his dances
were regulated by a consciousness of his group. It is
in the life of the primitive man that we recognize the tre-
mendous power of the dance as a socializing influence.
It is still largely instinctive and spontaneous, but it is
serious and utilitarian, and above all religious and social.
The dance is not entered into for its more superficial
advantages such as the grace and beauty it gives to the
dancer or the pleasure it gives to the observer. These
æsthetic qualities existed no doubt in early man's art,
but he did not yet have appreciation enough of these
values to pursue them for their own sake. In these early
human societies the dance derived its major importance
from its function as an integral part of their social life—
always closely associated with religion both as a means
of communication and as a means of expression of primitive man's reaction to the world of which he was beginning
to become more and more conscious. It was but natural
that these dances dealt very directly with all the different
phases of the life of that period. Every important event

in the life cycle of the individual was celebrated and symbolized in the use of bodily movement. The result is a considerable variety of dances that have been summed up into three groups; the religious dances; the dramatic or historic presentations of love and war; and the imitation dances, generally devoted to the mimicry of animals and of the forces of nature.

Gradually out of this savage and primitive stage man became civilized. He became more and more conscious of his environment and those about him as group and individual differentiations appeared. He gained in experience and power of reflection. He became more enlightened. And again we find this change reflected in the dance. Social conditions became such that the need for the former socializing influence of the dance was no longer apparent. Consequently, since man did not yet possess the abstract intelligence to rediscover new values and meanings for the dance, it was allowed to lose its place of social importance, to which it had owed its power in more primitive times. Moreover, man was finding other means besides bodily movements with which to express himself and to communicate his thoughts. Music and poetry were becoming the language of the emotions. The dance still persisted, but it was not the same dance. As the mental life increased in complexity, it began to dominate the emotions. The result is that in the dances of early ancient civilizations, especially of the Orient, the tendency to excessive emotion came to be curbed. In fact, emotion was practically subordinated, leaving the dance more moderate, more beautiful in form, still rich in meaning, but so fraught with symbolism that special knowledge was necessary to catch its significance. What had happened was that as man had become civilized, the dance had become an art.

The value of the dance in individual education, although manifesting itself throughout the lower stages of human development, was not to be fully realized until the later stages of culture. For like all other arts we find that the dance has fluctuated in importance in the social life of the people, according to the prevailing ideas and circumstances of the time. So when we come to the highly developed civilization of the ancient Greeks, we find the dance again playing an important rôle in human life, but what was once instinctive and random now became a deliberate feature of a philosophic scheme of education. The Greek point of view held that life in this world was all that mattered, and that it should be lived as abundantly and beautifully as was humanly possible. It was the philosophy of "eat, drink and be merry" at its best. The philosophic Greeks had none of the Christian fear of God. As to a hereafter, they trusted that to the future. They worshipped beauty and sought beauty in every phase of their mental, emotional and physical life, but their ideal was that in nothing should man go to excess. All that an enlightened man did was to be tempered by a most delicate appreciation of taste and moderation. Especially did the Greeks reverence the beauty of the human form. Its perfect development was to them an expression of the soul within, and the dance was the just embodiment of its rhythms. It was not only a means of experiencing, but also of putting into practice the laws of harmony, proportion, balance, and rhythm, which were the very foundation of their moral life. So to the Greek of the age of Pericles life in itself became an art, for he was ever seeking proportionate and harmonious relations in all that he was capable of thinking, feeling and doing. The place that the dance would hold in such a civilization is obvious. Not only was it deemed essential to the development of taste and refinement, but it was also considered a necessary part of their military and religious training. For a citizen to be well educated he must sing and dance well, and to sing and dance well meant to sing and dance only that which is good. Consequently, the dance was regarded as one of the best of aids to man's development. It was reverenced as an expressive form of art that at once expressed and enriched man's spirit.

Of course, such a conception as this could be the fruit only of the philosophy of the enlightened few, an ideal to be realized only in the lives of the best and finest, who through the working of a long-established tradition of mental and spiritual refinement had become attuned to its spirit. Such an ideal as this disseminated among the masses or transplanted to foreign soil is doomed to perish. As we pass from the best of Greek civilization down through its decline into the Roman period, we see that this is what happened. When the Romans in the course of their conquests came into contact with Greek civilization, they were much impressed by its elegance. To them it was all very novel and interesting, for art had long flourished in Greece, while primitive Rome was still barbaric. So they coveted the riches of Greek culture and tried to make them their own. But all Greek art was the fruit of a philosophy and a moral attitude toward life which the Roman could neither understand nor appreciate. The fundamental difficulty was that the Greek view of life was æsthetic, and the Roman was not. As a result, the ideal exaltation of bodily power of the Greeks became in the hands of the Romans mere licentiousness. The dance became a mere source of entertainment, indulged in simply for the delight it brought to the senses. The Romans did not find in the human form a revelation of the spiritual realm; they saw only the body in the body.

Moreover, the dance which the Romans cultivated was not a dance peculiar to themselves which they had themselves evolved; it was a dance that was peculiar to the development of another people. It was in no way an expression of the Roman spirit, nor was its beauty such as the Roman populace could understand. Consequently, the Roman dances at best were but a degenerate form of the Greek dances. As the moral level of the people sank, the dance was dragged down with it. So debased did the dance become that it was looked down upon by the Roman philosophers as an amusement unfit for the cultured. Even though theatrical dancing reached a high stage of perfection among the Romans, dancing as an art fell with the decay of this civilization. But the fault did not lie in the dance. It was the use made of it. Because movement so quickly and truthfully reflects feeling, it has always been a mirror of the moral attitude of peoples. Just as language may be expressive either of vulgar or refined thought and feeling, so movement may be either fine or crude.

From the decline of the Roman civilization we pass to the Christian era where we are confronted with a complete change in philosophy. The emphasis had been transferred from this world to the life of the hereafter. The paramount consideration of all living was the saving of the soul. Therefore since the body was looked upon as a hindrance to the soul, it must be ignored. It must be punished and bruised in order to exalt the soul. Anything that expressed the livelier feelings of instinctive human nature or in any way suggested the former pagan sense of life was at once banished by this ascetic belief into the realm of wickedness. Naturally the dance was too much of a pleasure to be suffered in secular life, but it was permitted to exist in a very staid form as part of the ritual of worship.

In the middle ages the dance flourished under the auspices of chivalry, and became an important part of the masquerades and balls of the courts. Among the masses, it came to play a prominent part in all rural festivities, and in the celebrations of the villages and towns, it later achieved prominence in the morality play. From these sources the dance may be said to have taken on two distinct forms—one the highly conventional form followed by the members of the courts and later by the professional dancers, and the other the freer, more expressive and more symbolic form which grew up among the folk of the various countries.

From the former line comes the ballet (whose history in itself would fill a book) and such familiar forms as the gavotte and passe-pied, and later, the waltz, polonaise, polka, and mazurka. The important thing to note about these conventionalized forms is that they are artificial in the sense that they are taught by inventive dancing masters, that they call for small, nice movements, rather than large instinctive ones, and that many of the movements especially in the case of the ballet, call for positions which are in opposition to the natural laws of bodily movement. It should be noted also that these forms tended to arouse an interest in technique rather than spirit—a tendency which has since caused the decline of the ballet—and that they demanded for their mastery longer periods of study than could be given by the average person. The explanation of these forms lies in the fact that the costumes of the habitués of the court did not allow for any freer movements, and that their custom of doing nothing left them bored and avid of novel entertainment from the efforts of others. Then, too, the wealth of the nobility permitted the long periods of study; but their habits of living failed to enrich their spirit to the point where they could appreciate sincerity of expression above exceedingly skillful technique. The results of these conditions was what always happens when those who dance lose their conception of the dance as an art and exploit or degrade its technique. The dance degenerated in form and lost its hold on public esteem.

But parallel with the development of the ballet and other conventional forms had grown up the folk dances. These are more directly descended from the dances of ancient times. They are the expression of a people who have labored, and fought, and loved, and lived together and who, still having an unhampered self-consciousness, instinctively express their common joys and sorrows by natural, rhythmical movement. Since one or another of these dances is familiar to almost everyone, it is necessary to note here only a few of their more important characteristics. In the first place they differ from the court dances and keep nearer to the direct line of descent in that they have sprung from the people as an expression of everyday life, as a representation of the work and the beliefs of the great mass of each nation. While their form is as exact in its own way as that of the early court dances, and while each generation has to learn them from the preceding one, the movements are more natural, allowing for greater abandonment and freedom of expression in the action. They give the spirit full play without any abnormal premium on formal technique. Where the other dances are in and of themselves merely pleasing, artistic forms, these dances are full of life and vitality. But as the people became more educated and more commercial, they lost much of this fine spirit of folk unity with the result that the old folk dance forms failed to spread to the newer countries. It is only comparatively recently therefore, that the true value of folk dancing has been recognized in America, for instance, and it is only now that the old folk dances are beginning to be taught.

The United States has no dances of its own, no dances which are expressive of the race which is an amalgamation of all races, no dances which are truly American. Each race has its dance, but there has been no dance to express the spirit of the race to which all these others have together given birth. Neither have there been any artificial dances which were the heritage of all. In fact, in America, the fortunes of the dance have, until recently, been poor. There was in the beginning, especially in the North, practically no dancing because of Puritan influence. Later the square dances, the waltz, and the popular English folk dances entered through the more liberal settlements of the South. For many years, however, especially since the introduction of jazz from South America, there has been no popular form of dancing that is in any sense artistic. Of course, there have been schools of "fancy" dancing of one kind and another and schools of the ballet, but the number of people who could take advantage of these schools was necessarily limited.

About 1900 the reaction against artificial and sterile forms set in, and soon after that time the movement was started to lead the people back to the Greek ideal of dancing—that is to movement founded on the laws of natural motion and rhythm. It began in private studios, but it is gradually finding its way into the colleges and public schools of the country. It should not be thought that the new dancing is essentially Greek in theme or action. If it were merely an effort to reproduce Greek dancing, it could expect no better success than the Romans achieved with their effort to imitate a foreign art. The leaders of this movement have gone to the Greeks not because they are patterns to be slavishly imitated, but because they, whose artistic achievements have never been surpassed, accorded so high a place to the dance in the education of their youth. From the Greeks the leaders of the movement have learned again the educational value of dancing, and a technique which is based on natural rather than unnatural positions of the body. They realize, however, that as the Greeks used their dances to express their own reaction to the life of their time, so we of the twentieth century must dance the life of our age. For our themes we may at times return to the Greeks, since they understood so fully the meaning of life and so poetically and so beautifully interpreted its great forces. As we dance to-day, however, we should express our own conception of the thought which the Greek word or legend but symbolizes. Therefore, although we have adopted the Greek ideal of dancing, we are adapting it to the needs of modern people in a modern world. The great emotions which are the themes of so many of our dances now as then are, of course, to be found in all ages. The manner of expressing them will, however, differ from age to age; so even though we dance under the inspiration of the Greeks, our dances will be very different from those that were danced in the days of Plato.

We have seen that throughout history every age of great intellectual activity has brought a fresh development of the dance. So it is not surprising that in this age of free intellectual activity we too are experiencing a renewed interest in the dance. It is well, however, to note what the claims of the dance are upon the interest of the present. The dance is no longer the only means of æsthetic expression. It has many rivals in both the fields of art and recreation. Because it has so often been exploited and degraded, it still frequently, even in its highest form, meets with indifference or even opposition. Nevertheless, increasing numbers of people are to-day desirous of living as abundantly as possible, and are eager for all the things that go to enrich life. They are, therefore, scrutinizing the dance for its qualifications as a physical activity, as an educational opportunity, as a social force, as an art. In other words, they are asking what place can be given to the dance in this rushing modern world.

The purpose of this whole discussion is to bring out the fact that in order to evolve the dance as an art in the individual it should be developed along the lines of its racial evolution. At first as we have seen, it was crude, instinctive and expressive of exuberant life. Gradually,

Photo by Geo. Bell, Milwaukee, Wis.   Courtesy of Woodley Studio, Madison, Wis.

by laws of his own nature, man learned to master the working material of his medium, and was led on to higher planes of conscious expression. To wisely direct this evolution in the student we must appreciate wherein the constructive values of artistic endeavor lie and what conditions they operate.

by laws of his own nature, man learned to master the working material of his medium, and was led on to higher planes of conscious expression. To wholly direct this evolution in the student we must appreciate wherein the constructive values of artistic endeavor lie and what conditions they operate.

Chapter III

THE DANCE IN THE CURRICULUM

Before we consider the dance as a part of the course of study in school or college, we must be sure that we know what we mean when we use the term "education." There are, and probably always will be, many different theories of education. If we go to one of the first masters of educational theory, Plato, we find that "the purpose of education is to give to the body and soul all the beauty and all the perfection of which they are capable." This definition of purpose still holds in its essentials, but to-day we should probably qualify it in some such direction as that suggested by Spencer's definition of life as "the conscious adjustment of internal relations to external." This definition implies self-activity, and that we may take as the keynote of current educational theory. Everywhere educators are realizing perhaps more clearly than ever before that what we need in our schools is more skillful stimulation to self-activity and less pedagogical preaching. The aim of all modern education is the freest and fullest development of the individual based upon a scientific understanding of his physical, mental, spiritual, and social needs. We know now, that knowledge is not something residing outside of the child, that may be imported into his system but that it is the result of his personal

contact with the world about him. Consequently, we seek to educate the child by giving him opportunities to develop himself. And in so doing, we try to meet his individual interests because we realize that they yield us the key to his needs and his capacities. Education cannot give the individual capacities, which must be inborn, but it can stimulate and help them both to unfold and to develop.

Of all these needs of man, one of the most fundamental is his need of some way to express his emotional reaction to life. That means an art form. Now of all the art forms known to man, the dance is the most available, since every man finds his instrument ready for his purpose in his own body. Anyone who knows how can create his dance for himself, and so satisfy to some extent, at least, his latent desire to create that which is pleasing in rhythm and form without dependence on any external agency. Or if he wants a more social pleasure, he will again find the dance about the readiest means of gratifying his wish. In a true democracy this opportunity to realize his fullest self, to laugh, to create, to enjoy the beautiful, to feel himself in harmony with the rhythm of the universe—should be given to every individual, especially to every child. In the "old country" the folk dances met this requirement to a certain extent, but in America, presumably the most democratic of all nations, the only solution of the problem available has been the one-step and the fox-trot, enjoyable in their way but admittedly not dances of any marked beauty or capability of satisfying the creative instinct. It is to remedy this condition that those interested in the revival of the dance have worked to restore to the people that which is their rightful heritage—a dance form which is both artistic and expressive, social and creative.

That it will prove to be a greater art in the hands of some than in the hands of others is obvious, but as every child has a right to a box of crayons and certain instruction in the fundamental principles of the art of drawing, whether there is any chance of his ever becoming a great artist or not, so every child has a right to know how to obtain control of his body so that he may use it, to the limit of his abilities, for the expression of his reactions to life. And even if he can never carry his efforts in this direction as far as the actual dance, he may experience the sheer joy of free and rhythmic movement, an addition to life to which every human being is entitled.

Moreover, as has been suggested in the course of the foregoing discussion, the dance is peculiarly adapted to the purposes of education. It serves all the ends of education—it helps to develop the body, to cultivate the love and appreciation of beauty, to stimulate the imagination and challenge the intellect, to deepen and refine the emotional life, and to broaden the social capacities of the individual that he may at once profit from and serve the greater world without.

But it is obvious that if the dance is to realize these possibilities it must take upon itself a form that is natural and educational. It must base its movements on the laws of bodily motion; its technique must be simple enough to afford to those who have comparatively little time to study the dance, an adequate mastery of their medium of expression—the body—and complex enough to prove interesting and valuable to the student who wishes to make the dance his chosen art. The scope of its rhythm must be broad enough to include the various rhythms of the dancers; and it must be flexible enough in forms and content to provide opportunity for widely different types of individuals to express themselves. If it is to be truly educational, it must be elastic so that the growth of the individual will be slow enough to achieve completeness. Above all, it must be grounded on definite principles and directed toward a carefully conceived goal.

The type of dancing, then, is educational which promotes the growth of the individual, which stimulates him to creative thought and activity, and which aims to give him the mental, physical, and spiritual poise which will enable him "to appreciate and meet the demands of life effectively." It is in its broadest sense, therefore, that the word *dancing* is here used. It includes many things—posture, gesture, pantomime, symbolism expressed by the body in its various members or in its totality, and self-abandonment and recreative pleasure. The dance, according to this definition is the sincere and spontaneous expression of a thought or feeling, presented not because the dancer wished to attract attention or make a sensation, but because he has something which he really wants to express. It is emotional self-expression through rhythmical movement.

There is nothing really new in this type of dancing. There are few really new elements in the world. All creative thinking or creative working is but the fresh commingling of old elements in new ways which are better suited to the ever changing needs of men. As man evolves, he modifies and adds to the old, using now less of one element, now more of another. When these changes in proportion are made intelligently, we have genuine progress. So it is the purpose of all educational activities that are worthy of the name to help people to use these eternal elements intelligently with due regard to the needs and aspirations of mankind. For it is only in the light of its effects on human personality that any effort has meaning for human beings.

Obviously, the teacher of educational dancing, if she is to make the most of her opportunities, must pay more attention to the peculiar characteristics of the individual student than is usually possible in ordinary dancing classes. She must try to discover within each one of her students that innate rhythm that, whether he will or no, whether he be even conscious of its presence or not, is forever demanding a harmonious unity between thought, and feeling, and action. It is upon what her students actually *are*, both spiritually and physically, that she must build her work. This necessity of adaptation to the individual makes the problem of organization into classes,—always a serious enough problem in any educational undertaking,—doubly acute. For this form of dancing being primarily democratic—as it must be if it is to fulfill its educational purposes in the public school curriculum—will attract all kinds of children, the shy, the bold, the ultra-self conscious, those who have naturally a fine sense of rhythm, those who have not, those who have plenty of imagination and originality, those who have had what little they may have been born with completely trained out of them. Such discrepanices in natural endowment and training form a serious problem for work that depends for its very justification on its ability to meet the needs of each individual. So far as the younger students are concerned, the problem is best solved where the amount of technical work studied is about the same, if children of about the same age are grouped together, for then the fund of experience to which the teacher can appeal will be about the same in each case.

With the older students, especially with college students, the question of age is no longer so important, and it becomes more a question of technique and responsiveness. There does, however, arise even here the question of where to place the student whose technique is not well developed but who has a very keen appreciation of the spirit of the dance and who is very well developed intellectually, dramatically, and emotionally. On the whole, it has been found wiser to let such students go into the advanced or intermediate classes. If they are kept with the less advanced workers too long, their interest is likely to wane, while if they are advanced, they are receiving constant inspiration from the other dancers. As a rule, such students become eager to work on their technique outside of class in order that their dancing may do justice to what they really feel.

Practical details of number of students in each class and number of meetings a week, and so on, will vary of course with the organization of which the dancing class is a part. The following suggestions bear upon those problems which confront the teacher in the college or university where dancing is a part of the physical education program. For effective work, the dancing class should meet at least twice a week. It is also well for students to have access to a room with a Victrola sometime between meetings of the class in order that the more ambitious may have a chance to progress and the slower may have a chance to catch up with what has already been done in class. The dancing period itself, since the neuro-muscular readjustments necessary to work of this type take time, should be, at least, forty to sixty minutes long. The actual size of the class will have to vary, of course, with the amount of floor space available, but the best results will be obtained if it is not allowed to exceed thirty. More can be handled, of course, but it is very difficult for the teacher to give the necessary individual attention to a larger number.

Whatever the class, whether it be one of beginners or of advanced students preparing to go out to teach the dance themselves, it will find its work more congenial and more stimulating if it can carry it on in surroundings that are harmonious with the spirit of the dance. In teaching dancing as an art, therefore, the teacher will work to create such an artistic atmosphere that the students will naturally and easily overcome needless inhibitions of shyness and self-consciousness and rise above themselves into a complete absorption in their art. A bright, airy room with a smooth, clean floor is a necessity. But if it is hung with curtains in some soft, warm, shade that affords a versatile background for dance groups, it may become a very real help to the creation of that spirit of beauty that is one of the aims of such a class. It is not at all a bad idea for the students themselves to undertake the furnishing of their dance room. They may with much enjoyment of the process, earn the money for the Victrola that so much facilitates their work, and for any other things that may add serviceableness or beauty to their surroundings.

The same principles apply to the choice of costume for the dancing class. If it is absolutely necessary, as it often is in the lower grades in the public schools, much of the work, although not all of it, can be done in regular school clothes. But that is unfortunate, for the dance deserves the consideration of a special costume as much as swimming or gymnastics. Indeed, the opportunity to enjoy graceful line and color in costume is part of the experience.

With the less advanced classes where taste is as yet untried it is better to have fewer choices of design but freedom in choice of color. In the more advanced classes the students can exercise their individual taste in design. They should be reminded that the same costume is not necessarily equally becoming to everyone; it is a worthwhile and interesting problem to encourage the students to consider the different kinds of costumes before deciding upon the one they may wish to make. In the accompanying plates several costumes are suggested which have proved quite universally becoming and attractive, and which may serve as models until further experience will suggest others.[1] The designs given are simple and with a little ingenious adjustment can be given an entirely different effect. For general class work the short costumes are the more suitable, but there are times when a long costume is desirable. Taste and interest may be stimulated by discussing the various lengths and colors of costumes that would be most appropriate for the different dances studied, were they to be properly costumed. Long costumes are very effective both in motion and rest but their success depends somewhat upon the material used. It should be sheer, soft, and of a quality that will drape well and hang in easy folds. Silk and cotton crêpe

[1] See plates, pages 233-243.

is an inexpensive material that lends itself readily to draping. It usually comes, however, only in 36 in. width which limits its use to those costumes requiring this width. Tricolette (fibre silk), crêpe de chine, and chiffons are materials that are useful for practically all kinds of costumes. Costumes should not be hemmed as a hem usually destroys the natural hang of the draping. Should the cut edge fray it is best to have it picoted. When the edges of the neck and armholes are cut they should be reinforced in some way, as with two or three rows of hem-stitching or by a rolled hem.

As a rule, especially in the public schools, there should be a feeling against unnecessarily expensive costumes for classroom work. At the same time, however, time and effort should be given in having the costumes artistic and becoming no matter how inexpensive the material or how simple the line. Further charm can be gained without much added expense by tieing and dyeing the materials. Cheese cloth when effectively dyed makes up into very satisfactory costumes. Most libraries have books on dyeing which are readily obtainable for those who care to read up on it, or it is often possible to secure help with costumes both in designing and dyeing from the Home Economics Department of school or college.

It is advisable if possible to dance bare-footed, but this does not mean that the work is to be called bare-foot dancing. Costume has nothing to do with educational dancing. But even where one dances bare-footed, some protection is needed for practicing turns on the floor, especially if the feet are tender. Stockings should never be worn without sandals, as they are very uncertain and dangerous because of their tendency to slip. Sandals with a heel and toe such as are represented in the plate are very satisfactory and practical.

The costumes of the dancing class can be made a very real source of beauty and enjoyment. But while like artistic surroundings they help to create the right atmosphere for the dance, they are in no way indispensable to it. They must never be suffered to encroach on the attention that should be devoted to the dance itself, or to assume an importance that makes the dancer feel in any way dependent upon them.

In order that the class may approach the work in the best spirit, this dancing should be elective. Even then there will be variety enough of purpose in the group that assembles for the first meeting of the beginning class. There will be the inevitable proportion of those who are trying to satisfy requirements without any great concern about the means, there will be some who will have been drawn by curiosity, and then there will be a majority who will have come for any one of several good reasons. Some will be anxious for training that may help them to become better social dancers, others will be seeking an outlet for their energies and a new source of recreation, and still others will come for the sake of harmonious physical development and poise.

The teacher's first task will be to arouse the interest of this heterogeneous group. It is helpful to make clear at the first meeting of the class the purpose and the values of the work. There may be students in the class who have been accustomed to learn dancing by paying other people to think for them in their dancing. Unless they can change their point of view, they will be disappointed in the work. The whole class should be made to feel at the start that the important thing in this class is what they can do for themselves, that their progress will depend upon what they put into the work. This means that the class will be something more than what one person makes it. For if students are encouraged to help plan the work, they will be eager to bring their own originality and initiative to bear upon the subject in hand. And if the teacher herself will set them the example by bringing in the new ideas and suggestions which she picks up in her reading, or in the lectures she attends, or in any of her daily contacts, the students will enjoy bringing in suggestions from their outside experience and applying to the problems of the dance the resources they have acquired from their other studies. The resulting class work will be something far more rich and vital than any mapped-out course.

And on the other hand if students have a real understanding of the work and a sense of playing an essential part in it, they will be glad to supplement their class work by individual practise outside of class hours. University students of the dance often take their fundamental exercises home, and not only practise them, but get their friends to join them. The normal human being may be counted upon to enjoy vigorous bodily exercise, especially if there are added to it the satisfactions of rhythmical movement and group participation in a common activity.

When it comes to planning the course of dancing for the school or college, the teacher will be confronted with a distressing lack of background and preparation for the work on the part of her students. She will have to build up the background that her work needs while she is carrying on the work itself. To do this successfully, she must have an abundance of resources to draw upon herself.

First of all, she must remember and see that her students remember that any art has two aspects, and that it must be considered in two very intimately related but still, for pedagogical purposes, very distinct ways. The more general way involves the study of those principles that underlie it as an art—that relate it to the whole field of art, and the second and more particular, requires the mastery of the particular rules and laws of its special technique that distinguish it from all other forms of art. From the first point of view it is an art; from the second, a craft. There can, of course, be no question as to where its glory lies, but no art can ever realize its finest possibilities as an art, unless it is soundly based on a mastery of its craft.

The teacher of educational dancing will go far abroad into history, into psychology, into philosophy, and into art, for those conceptions of man's fundamental needs and possibilities that will constitute the heart of her artistic purpose. But she will base all her endeavors on a very thorough understanding of her particular craft. She must have not only faith in her work but also a sound knowledge of its fundamental principles, and of those portions of other fields upon which they are grounded. She must not only be filled with enthusiasm for the art of dancing, but she must have a firm and thorough grasp of the science of dancing. It is the science that enables her to organize her work intelligently, for it is science that tells one how to adjust the means to the end, how to go to work. That is the aim of all technique, the accomplishment of preconceived purposes with economy of effort.

The medium of the dance is the body. The first task of the dancer who is to express his thoughts and feelings by means of his body is to make that body sensitive and responsive to the demands he is later to make upon it. The teacher must then be thoroughly conversant with the physical mechanism of the body. She must understand the functions of its various parts, and she must appreciate their relation to the whole. In order to be able to help her students acquire the greatest degree of flexibility and responsiveness in all the parts employed in the dance she must have accurate knowledge of the complete range of movement in the joint-muscle mechanism. All of this obviously requires a thorough knowledge of anatomy, kinesiology, and physics.

The "course" in educational dancing will begin then with the effort to master the body as an instrument of expression. During this part of the study the first aim of the exercises used is to establish habits of muscular guidance and control in order that the student may have full use of his instrument free from hampering limitations. These exercises are based on the natural movements of the human animal and are in themselves the systematic application of the laws of the joint-muscle mechanism. Since they lay the foundation of this type of dancing, they will be hereafter referred to as the "fundamentals." They consist of a series of movements which in themselves exact fundamental coördinations, varying from the simple to complex. The majority of them are composed of movements which begin in the spine and extend from the simple to the more complex and difficult

in a well-ordered progression to all the smaller muscle
groups of both extremities of the body. Because of the
muscular activity involved in the upright position many
of the fundamentals are executed lying on the floor, with
the pull of gravity at a minimum. When the fundamental
principles of movement have been mastered by the pupils
in this position, the next step is for them to carry these
principles over into the upright position, adding the co-
ordination of the muscles which support us when standing. At first every movement must be under conscious
control and must be the object of attention, or otherwise
the correct habits would not be established. Later when
these are mastered, the student can afford to trust to his
impulses and devote his attention to the content of the
dance.

The student has now come to know his means of expression. The next step is locomotion or movement upon
the feet. The essence of the problem is the transference
of the weight of the body from one foot to the other,
from one to both, or from both to both, as illustrated in
walking, running, leaping, skipping, sliding and hopping.
These are the elemental forms or the units of more complicated steps. We may compare this use of movement,
steps, gestures and so on, in expression to the knowledge
of words and their later combinations for expressive
uses. We are taught the use, values and meanings of
words, but when we come to tell a story, develop a theme,
or express a thought we do not all use the same words nor
in the same combinations. What we do is to choose those
words in our vocabulary which will most completely embody and set forth our thoughts and feelings. So in dancing, the students should be so taught as to give expression

to their own reactions and not those of another. Here it seems, is where much of the dancing taught fails almost entirely to be educational. It is at best an imitative process, a type of work which does not grow out of any creative germ. It is destructive to any stimulus for originality. It is mechanical, an application, not a creation.

These fundamentals are not dancing, and it is wiser not to call the classes in fundamentals, dancing, since there are students who will be disappointed if they spend many hours in so-called dancing classes without learning any dances. On the other hand, these fundamentals should be respected as a part of the technique of the subject, as a means of preparation and reënforcement of bodily control, and as an indispensable step toward acquiring a greater power of expression. In no way should they be regarded merely as an end in themselves or as a task set by the teacher. As a matter of fact the teacher need not worry about the interest of her class in any amount of preliminary work if she takes care to let them know just what they are doing and why, if she gives them a sense of direction and the immeasurable satisfaction of knowing that their most rudimentary efforts are making progress toward their goal.

A simple device for stimulating the student to perfect his mastery of the fundamentals has been found in the use of cards upon which the student's progress can be checked every so often, and his general proficiency estimated.[2] It is a convenient way of helping the student to discover just where he has reached his goal, and where he has fallen short, and of showing how he may work in

[2] For suggested form, see pages 292–293.

the future with greater economy and efficiency of effort toward his conquest of muscle wisdom.

By this time the student has achieved a fair degree of mastery of the elemental steps. He is now ready to combine them into more intricate movements, and to discriminate their capacities for expression. Balloons and scarfs often prove helpful at this stage, especially in the development of the finer points of bodily control. They lure the student on to activity, and by their movement suggest movements to him. Since this does not require too concentrated an effort, the body of the dancer is left free to respond. The balloons are very helpful as an objective when lifting the body off the floor—that is, in leaping with chest elevated to reach the balloon. The scarfs are especially good for the spiral taken in the upright position and also for leaping. Novel and delightful movements may result from this work to interest and stimulate the student.

But this is still not dancing. To the onlooker it may seem as if it were, for the movements and steps are well balanced and skillfully woven into evolutions. But the point is that these activities are all motivated entirely by the will. They are the result of conscious knowledge, working out what reason tells us is possible. They are in no sense the spontaneous and peculiarly individual expression of the dancer's own mind, feelings, or creative impulses. It is through this study, however, that the student is discovering his own possibilities, and trying out for himself the feeling of different rhythmic combinations. In short, he is building up a vocabulary of steps with which he will later express himself.

Meanwhile, he is learning to make use of the greatest

of all the aids to the dance, music. The problems involved in the use of music for the dance will be considered later in their appropriate place. It will be noted here, however, that music is always used with the exercises. For the music both gives them emotional content, making them more far-reaching in their effect and acts as a regulating and stimulating force.

On the other hand, in preparation for the dance proper, the teacher will constantly endeavor to give the student a deeper appreciation of music by explaining something of its nature, its technique, and its history. And she will try to bring the student to enter into the spirit and meaning of particular pieces. Music has gathered up so much of life's experience that the dancer who can understand its language may find in it inexhaustible inspiration. Moreover music, having been born of man's emotions, is ever capable of arousing them again. So from music the student may obtain beautiful emotional themes to retranslate into movement; music becomes the auxiliary of the dance—suggesting and regulating its evolutions.

In all this preliminary work it is wise to encourage the students to "make haste slowly." Especially should those students who learn slowly be given plenty of time. If the rhythm of the music is not clear, the student should feel that it is the expected thing for him to stop and go through the preliminary steps again until he really "has it." Or if in the case of an exercise, the spiral, for instance, requires more control of the back than he has as yet obtained, he should not feel in the least disgraced or "put back" because the teacher suggests that he work with a less advanced class until he has had time to review some of the preliminary exercises before attempting the more complex and difficult ones. Often the teacher may help a backward student to master the exercise on which the class is working by actually putting him through the movement. In this way the student obtains the correct kinesthetic sensations so that he can gauge his subsequent movements accordingly. The beginner who is doing the work incorrectly should never have his faults called attention to as self-consciousness is apt to result from such a practice. If several students are making the same mistake, an explanation of the exercise and a general warning against common mistakes will prove helpful, for the students who need these suggestions and are ready to use them advantageously will take them. If only one or two members of the class are working incorrectly, the teacher can quietly help them individually. It is never wise in any case to insist that a student take suggestions, however helpful they may be, before he is able to accept them without confusion.

The student is now ready to begin to dance. Because one cannot very well think of form and movement when he is actually dancing, it is usually advisable to divide the class period at this stage into two parts. In this way some of the time can be given to developing the control of that part of the body which is especially used in the dance given in the last part. By following this method, it is possible to establish the correct kinesthetic sensations and at the same time so strengthen the sense of form that when the student is dancing, these technical matters can be adequately cared for by the sub-conscious. In this way the student has absolute freedom of expression and yet runs no danger of falling into harmful positions—a danger which is very real when one has not both the knowledge and habit of correct movement. Another advantage of such a method is that the nerve centers and muscular masses of that part of the body on which the student has been particularly working, (always keeping in mind its relation to the whole) have been aroused so that they respond naturally and appropriately to the music. It is then easier for the individual to give himself over to the music and throw himself completely into the dance. Although in its most advanced form, the dance is a pure expression of the dancer's own thought and feeling, a creative act in the most literal sense of the term, it is usually wise in teaching elementary classes to suggest the content of the dance. Such a suggestion serves to arouse the emotions of the student, and at the same time gives him an opportunity to think out his material before attempting to build the dance. The teacher may do this by reading some verse, or by telling a brief story and explaining carefully any symbolism involved. In either event the material given should not be too detailed, but should be composed of the main outlines only in order that the student may use his own imagination and experience in creating the dance interpretation of the words. To ask the average student to create the themes as well as the dance is to ask him to take two steps at once. On the other hand not to give him some opportunity to create the dance entirely, especially in the more advanced work, is to defeat the aims of this type of dancing by thwarting the growth of the student's imagination through lack of exercise. The balance between too much and too little exercise of the imagination, like exercise of the body, must be nicely kept. The average teacher needs also to guard against her natural desire to have the dance embody her dreams and ideas. If the student is let alone he may evolve a version of his own that will be quite as lovely as his teacher's, and, what is more to the point, far more expressive. In any event, the dance that the student evolves will be of greater value to him, as well as of greater pleasure, than a dance dictated by someone else.

But in thus providing her student with the opportunity to dance his own interpretation of the music or story, it is important for the teacher to keep in mind the relative maturity or immaturity of each class, and the amount of experience-deepening material that she has already given them, so as to avoid the mistake of giving them material which is too difficult. No one can interpret a theme which he is incapable of conceiving, or whose implications and symbolism he cannot understand. This does not, of course, mean that a teacher should never give the students any material but that which they can interpret easily and spontaneously. A great deal of the material presented in this study, as in every other, is used in order that the student may discover his latent emotional, dramatic, and intellectual powers, and develop them. It is, however, necessary to avoid giving the students subjects that are so far in advance of their present state of development that it is necessary for them to overreach themselves, or to go through actions whose significance they do not really understand.

For this reason some effort at classification of students becomes imperative when we begin work on the dance itself. When we try to use movement for expressive purposes, we get into the realm of individual differences. In our emotional demands we must regard at once the student's capacity of feeling and his ability to express his feeling. In order to gain the interest and coöperation of the students in such a classification it has proved helpful to post a list of certain requirements that afford an objective basis for classification of students. As will be seen, this list proceeds from very elementary to fairly difficult movements.

Requirements for Dancing Try-Outs

Classification "C"

A. Muscular control based on accurate discrimination of the kinesthetic sense.
  1. First roll—taken with any of the following leads:
    a. upper back (head)
    b. lower back (hip)
    c. shoulder.
  2. Flexion and extension of back.
  3. Preliminary crawl or back flexion and extension with a moving base.
  4. Folding and unfolding.
  5. Coördination of shoulders and arms with the back.
B. Realization and appreciation of music through movement.
  1. Elementary steps.
  2. Combination of these into the waltz, polka, and schottische, and impromptu combinations.
  3. Phrasing based on accentuation, direction, and change of step and intensity.
C. All of the above carried over into the dancing of "Fanfare."

Classification " B "

A. Muscular control based on accurate discrimination of the kinesthetic sense.
  1. Any of "C."
  2. Second roll.
  3. Preliminary crawl forward and backward.
  4. Leg control.
  5. Leg and back coördination.
  6. The walk in good form.
  7. Localization and variation of leads with the body in locomotion.
B. Realization and appreciation of music through movement.
  1. Any of "C."
  2. "Slide and lift" carrying the free leg in back; "Slide and turn" with a leap.
  3. Phrasing based on response to:
    a. Kinesthetic sense of equilibrium and movement and direction;
    b. Localized phrasing taken by the arms or the spine;
    c. Association of ideas, imagination, and fancy;
    d. Structure of the music used.
C. All carried over into the dancing of "Bacchanale."

Classification " A "

A. Muscular control based on the kinesthetic sense.
  1. All the fundamentals with variations.
    a. 1st, 2nd, and 3rd roll;
    b. Folding and unfolding
    c. The completed crawl forward and backward.
  2. Dramatization of fundamentals.

Classification " A "—Cont.
  B. Realization and appreciation of movement.
    1. As in Class "C" and "B."
    2. An original rhythm forming a completed phrase.
    3. Improvisation.
  C. Two original dances, one of which must be comedy.

It is well to have these requirements posted a long time ahead in order that the students may study them and also that the teacher may refer to them in the class work. The students sign up for the classification for which they wish to try. These tests should not be regarded as an examination to trip up the students. They should be administered in a helpful spirit with the purpose of finding out what the student knows, as well as what he does not know. Consequently, only a small group should be taken at a time. Such a classification has always proved stimulating and interesting to the students, and the results have proved invaluable to the teacher when it comes to the organization of classes for the following term.

Some opportunity beyond the scheduled class work should be given those students who have the interest and the capacity to go faster and do more advanced work than is possible in the ordinary class. This is provided for at Wisconsin by a class that meets on Wednesday nights. Its membership is open to all those who wish to join and who have achieved sufficient mastery of the dance from both the technical and the artistic point of view to be able to contribute to the activity of the group and to profit from it. So the class draws into itself students with various contributions to make—in music, in words, in color and design, in acting. Consequently, it has come to be felt as an influential art center in the various activities of the campus. Yet it is in no way a chartered club with a pin. Indeed, the effort has been to avoid such an organization, because the members feel that the most fitting badge of the group is the way in which it affects thought and conduct. The result is a spirit which creates a much stronger and finer feeling of unity than any material pin could ever establish.

The name of this group is Orchesis. The significance of the name and of the organization which bears it is made clear at a simple yet beautiful ceremony for its reception of new members.

There is nothing secret about the class. The ritual is offered to anyone who wishes to use it, with the sole proviso that its true spirit be kept. Already there are several Orchesis groups at different universities, so that it seems the time may come when such an interest may be of considerable influence for the teaching of a high type of dancing in America.

The society devotes itself to original creative work—the recreation of music, poetry, myth, and legend into the movements of the dance, or the development of their own inventions. The members work among themselves with no thought of appealing to wider circles. From their regular work develop programs for "guest evenings" —informal recitals in which the students present their own dances to friends they have invited. And from these develops the larger program that is open to all who are interested. The proceeds of this evening have gone to help finance the various activities of the Women's Athletic Association at Wisconsin, and to a scholarship fund to assist some girl interested in the dance.

Because of the scant allotment of time that is usually given to the dance in programs of physical education, the external results of our work will sometimes fall short of our expectations. In such cases, we must encourage ourselves by the reflection that external results are not our goal and that our purposes do not depend for their justification upon the performance of our students. The teacher who makes finished performance her objective may secure more conventionally perfect dancing, but her influence on her students will be narrowing and stultifying. Truth and depth of artistic feeling are not to be gauged by external results. The aim of the teacher of educational dancing should be to develop the taste and appreciation of her students for all that is good and beautiful in art and life. In many ways work with such a purpose cannot bear its full fruit until later years. It is really for the future, even more than the present, that teaching such as this should build.

Chapter IV

THE FUNDAMENTALS OF MOVEMENT

 The body is the medium of expression, the instrument of the dance. If it is to be a satisfactory instrument, it must be as much at the command of the dancer, as the piano is at the command of the musician. It must be more sensitive and responsive than even the most finely tuned instrument if it is to respond instantaneously to every flicker of emotion in the dancer's mind, from lightest mirth to despair. Then only can the dancer be free really to express himself.

Obviously such a highly-developed state of responsiveness is possible only when the physical mechanism of the body has been thoroughly studied and mastered. It is the purpose, therefore, of this first stage of the work to achieve that mastery of the body as an instrument by bringing about the greatest degree of flexibility in all its parts and establishing habits of muscular guidance and control. Obviously, such an undertaking demands a technique that will adequately develop and coördinate in a harmonious functioning not only all parts of the body, but to no small extent, all parts of the body and the mind as well.

Such a technique must be founded on a thorough understanding of that remarkably ingenious mechanism of levers, axes of movement, joints, muscular organs of movement, and so on, that constitutes the human body, and a thorough mastery of the laws of natural movement. For the only movements that can effect the purposes of this type of dancing are those that afford the freest possible play to the natural motions of the individual body. Artificial movements achieved through imitation have little value for the student of educational dancing. What he needs are those natural movements that with use become so habitual as to be instinctive.

Unfortunately, the untrained movements of the average person of to-day are far from natural. It becomes necessary therefore to train the student back to being natural, to help him to free his body from useless and even harmful restrictions, and to restore to him that control upon which his freedom depends. It is for this purpose that the exercises to be described in this chapter have been devised. They are called the fundamentals because all further development of control and movement depends upon a thorough mastery of their basic importance. They consist of movements which in themselves demand fundamental coördinations. By no means do they exhaust all the possibilities of movement for the human body. Neither do they constitute any formula of lessons. They are rather to be regarded as a body of material from which a series of lessons for physical control may be arranged.

They offer the student abundant opportunity to develop sense of rhythm and feeling for movement. In many cases, new combinations can be worked out of these simpler movements with valuable experience for the student in developing a sense of form and a feeling for adaptive response. Ideas for fresh groupings will continually present themselves to the teacher, and the class, itself, in its impromptu work will often suggest still other combinations which the teacher can develop to give back to them in more available form.

In thus teaching the laws of balance and movement, the teacher who knows her physics, anatomy, and kinesiology will be able to give her students a more adequate conception of what they are doing. Students need to know why they are making movements if they are to make them with any intelligent appreciation of their value and possibilities. They will find this phase of their work more comprehensible and interesting if they have the use of muscle charts and, if possible, a skeleton.[1]

Students should early be taught to be critical of their own efforts, and resourceful in the invention of new and more effective ways of solving a given problem. Indeed, in all this work, the teacher should constantly encourage her students to lay hold of the various issues for themselves, and she should be most generous in her appreciation of invention.

This means, of course, that the work must be given in such a fashion as to allow the individual student to become acquainted with his own problems. He should be encouraged to study his own abilities, that he may discover his difficulties and strive to eliminate them. And, on the other hand, since each person has an entirely different set of bodily rhythms, he must become acquainted with them that he may be able to assimilate with his own rhythms those of any movement that he is studying.

[1] The "Frohse Anatomical Charts" are suggested. Address: A. J. Nystrom, Chicago, Illinois.

"For movements impress us as really graceful, only when we feel that their rhythm has been taken up voluntarily, that the dancer is free to throw it over whenever he wishes, and that even in its own power it still affords ample scope for individual whim and fancy."—*Souriau*.

At first every movement must be the object of conscious control and attention; otherwise the correct habits that will free our minds for higher purposes will not be established. Careful attention should also be given to the orderliness of movement. As soon as possible, some effort should be made to do the exercises with a feeling of building and phrasing—with an acceleration to the climax, and then an easing off of effort.

All this will mean unremitting attention and effort, but it is only in this way that the student will develop that sense of kinesthesia which is so essential to all effective use of the body. It has been defined by Blanton as "a consciousness of the amount or quickness of muscular exertion involved in the performance of a given act." It is this which makes possible that muscle memory that enables skill to reproduce intricate patterns of movement without conscious thought.

Here as elsewhere, music is of great service in the study of movement. But if it is to render its greatest service, it must always be of the best. For this purpose it should be melodious, soothing, with long phrasing and rhythms not too strongly marked. A few typical selections that are useful in general are Schubert's "Ave Maria," Kreisler's "The Old Refrain," Mendelssohn's "On Wings of Song," and Schubert's "Serenade." The following are a few selections that have proved useful for regulating back and arm movements:

Photo by Geo. Bell, Milwaukee, Wis.

Courtesy of Woodley Studio, Madison, Wis.

3/4—Waltz—Moderate tempo—
> Brahms, "No. 15,"
> Schubert, "Waltzes,"
> "Waltz for Balancing"
> Moszkowski, "Waltz in E,"
> Vigorous, "Faust Ballet Waltz," Gounod
> > "Faust Waltzes," Gounod.

4/4—Time—Slow—
> "Song of the Bargemen," arr. by Aldrich,
> "Chord Gasps," Schytte,
> "Deep River" (Negro Spiritual),

6/8—Moderate—
> Smooth and flowing—
> > "Slumber Song, " *Schumann*,
> > " 6/8 Rhythm for Sliding,"
> > "Schmetterling," *Merkel*,
> > "The Palms," *Faure*,
> Vigorous—"Sorrentina," *Lack*.

For further suggestions see the bibliography of music, pages 263–274.

After the students have gained a fair amount of control, and have established their own individual rhythms, the exercises may be regulated by the count or phrasing of the music used. It is also of advantage to change the time. For example, give back flexion and extension, or rotation, etc., to 2/4, 3/4, 4/4, and 6/8 time in turn, pointing out the changes in difficulty of control, and in feeling the result of shortening or lengthening of the time interval of execution. With the more advanced students many of the fundamentals may be also dramatized. This will afford many exceedingly interesting problems, the working out of which will carry the students far on their road to the dance.

To facilitate handling, the exercises are given in outline form, based on the following classification of the parts of the body:

1. The Trunk—whose position and movements depend upon movements possible in the spine.

2. The upper limbs or arms—whose movements are closely associated with and affected by the action of the shoulder girdle.

3. The lower limbs or legs—whose movements are affected by the action of the lumbar spine, and in turn affect the position of the pelvic girdle.

The position of the various exercises in the outline does not necessarily mean that they are to be studied in that particular order. While it should never be forgotten that parts belong together and work together only because of an existing whole, the outline in general follows the plan of studying parts first, and the body as a unit last. That is why the rolls and folding and unfolding come toward the end of the outline, although they may be given in the beginning lessons. This apparent anomaly is to be explained by the fact of the natural growth of an individual's control from crude attempts to smooth, highly coördinated movements. This growth takes place as the localized control becomes more highly developed, with the result that each succeeding attempt is different from the last in that it involves more and better control.

The development of all parts of the body is so essential to the development of the whole that it is sometimes difficult to know which part of the body to emphasize first—whether the shoulders, the arms, the legs, or the back. Several reasons make it seem both logical and wise to begin with the movements of the back. First of all, when we stop to consider our structure and realize that our movements are determined by our joint-muscle mechanism, the importance of the spine and its movements becomes evident. All the highly expressive movements and positions of the head, the chest, and the trunk are possible only because of the action of the spine. On the other hand, while arms and legs are usually, even in the undeveloped and untrained, exercised sufficiently, the back is seldom exercised enough for its good, and often is actually abused. Few people realize the value of a free, strong, and flexible back, in spite of its importance for all the movements of the legs and arms, and for the general activity and poise of the entire body.

Before considering the movements of the spine, it is well to review the essential points of its structure. The spinal column is made of a series of bones or vertebræ (twenty-four moveable and ten immoveable—sacrum and coccyx) piled one on top of the other. These form the central axis around which all the other parts are arranged. On the upper end of this axis is poised the head; below by indirect connection, through the shoulder and pelvic girdles, the arms and legs respectively, are joined to the spine. As the central axis, then, the spine is seen to be a most important factor in the formation of the skeleton of the trunk, and in the control of the movements of the whole body. It is well to point out further the natural curves of the spine, making their relation to posture clear, to explain the structure of the vertebræ in the different regions and to show how that structure effects the range and type of movement in these parts, and finally, to explain how through its connection with the ribs, the spine is concerned with the formation of the chest wall.

I. UPPER PART OF BODY.

In much of the so-called interpretative dancing, the tendency is to have the back either stiff or in hyper-extended positions, with the head forced into some conventional or obviously classical position. Such artificiality of expression destroys the value of dancing both as a physical activity and as an art. For this reason, it is important that the student gain an intelligent mastery of the various regions of the spine. When the spine is rendered flexible and strong, and brought under control, the upper body becomes free and responsive, especially the neck, so that the head is free to respond to the slightest change of feeling. The degree of this freedom is a sure and true index of coördination.

1. MOVEMENTS OF THE SPINE.
   A. Flexion and extension.
      a. The whole spine.
         (1). Sitting on the floor tailor fashion—spine relaxed—head dropped forward. Gradually raise chest higher and higher, at the same time bringing head up and back as far as possible. Relax and repeat. Check the movement at different stages

Upper Part of Body—Cont.

and discuss the relation of the resulting positions to good posture. This is a helpful way of starting beginning classes. The position is natural, so that they can easily experience movement in the spine without being too confused as to localization of parts. Explain how this position limits movement in the lower back. After the class is familiar with the action of the spine in this position, assume the following:

(2). On hands and knees.
The spine is now in a horizontal position, and all parts are free for complete movement. To avoid the tendency to bend elbows, turn hands out. Aim for complete flexion and extension of the whole spine. In practicing flexion and extension in this position, it is often helpful to suggest to the students that they are drawing an imaginary circle, in front with the chin. Repeat with hands turned in—permitting elbows to bend.
Take with free motion in the hips and knees. This permits a wide and free movement.

(3). Standing on knees.
Same. After control in lumbar spine has been mastered, repeat with pelvic control. Relax anterior neck muscles.

Upper Part of Body—Cont.

(4). Half kneeling.

Same.

(5). Sitting back on heels.

It is more difficult to control movement in the lower back because it is somewhat fixed by its position. The tendency will be to apply movement only to the parts of the spine that are free. Take as complete flexion and extension of whole spine as position will permit. Repeat with pelvic control.

(6). Take the position of the crawl as in Fig. 1, Plate XIII, page 252.

Because this is difficult on account of balance, it should not be given until the student has attained sufficient control of the spine.

(a). Take full extension of the spine, (see Fig. 4, Plate XIV, page 253) starting the movement in the cervical spine by lifting the face first.

(b). Bring back to complete extension, starting the movement in the middle of the back.

(c). Same, pulling the back up by starting the movement in the lower back.

(d). Repeat (a), (b), and (c) with hands clasped in back. Keep arms relaxed.

b. Localization of Parts.

Note the varying range of movement in the different parts.

Upper Part of Body—Cont.

(1). Flexion and extension of the cervical spine with the thoracic and lumbar spine held inactive.

(2). Flexion and extension of the thoracic spine with the lumbar and cervical spine inactive. Because of its middle position it is impossible to isolate the thoracic spine entirely. For complete flexion it is excellent help for a partner to offer resistance. It causes the worker to hunch or "bow" the back. Explain how the structure of the thorax limits the range of movement in this part of the spine.

(3). Flexion and extension of the cervical and thoracic spine with the lumbar spine fixed.

(a). Taking position of the second roll (Plate IX, Fig. 3, page 248) face up, press as much of the lower back as possible against the floor. In this position take flexion and extension of the rest of the spine. Change position to face down (Plate IX, Fig. 1). To correct hyper-extension in the lumbar spine, lift abdomen and upper part of thighs from the floor. Repeat flexion and extension of upper parts of spine—lifting chest and head high. (If possible, pads should be provided for elbows and knees whenever they support the weight of the

Upper Part of Body—Cont.

body for a prolonged length of time.) Special effort should be made to make clear the strategic position of the lumbar spine, the nature of its movement, the structure of the pelvic girdle in general, and the effect of movements in the lower back on the change of position in the pelvis. Point out that the sacrum is wedged between the two large hip bones, forming a fixed base for the upper and moveable spine. Therefore any movement of the pelvis of necessity causes a change in the position of the base of the spine. The control of the lumbar spine and pelvis is so important and essential to good posture and movement that its control should be assured before advanced work is permitted. Notice the coöperative action of abdominal muscles. As much time as is necessary should be given to the mastery of control of the spine, especially of the lumbar region. Localized control of the lumbar spine is further promoted by standing against the wall, with feet far enough away to permit the lumbar thoracic spine and the head to touch the wall. In this position

Upper Part of Body—Cont.

"hollow" the lower back (hyperextension), and notice that this movement causes the lumbar spine to curve away from the wall; then flatten (flexion) it against the wall. Notice the change of position of the pelvis.

Repeat standing **away** from the wall.

(b). Sitting on a chair with the thoracic and lumbar spine pressed against the back of the chair.

Be sure of good control in abdominal and lower back muscles. Relax anterior neck muscles.

(*1*). Full extension of thoracic and cervical spine with the lumbar pressed against back of chair. This limits somewhat the extension in the upper spine, but helps to localize it in the lower spine. Have class attend to the effort of the lumbar spine to leave the chair at a certain point of extension in the upper spine.

(*2*). Same, letting the lower back leave the chair when the pull comes, but permitting no more extension than necessary. Aim to localize the extension in the

Upper Part of Body—Cont.

thoracic spine. Suggest lifting the chest higher and higher. Have the students experience extreme hyper-extension once or twice that they may know what is incorrect. Explain clearly. Relax anterior neck muscles.

(*3*). Leaning forward without the back of the chair as a guide.

(c). On the floor.
Same.

(*1*). Sitting back on the heels.
Same.

(*2*). Half kneeling.
Same.

(*3*). Standing.
Same.

(All are taken with the lumbar spine held in good position. A test of control is the ability to make adjustments under new conditions.)

(4). Flexion and extension of the lumbar spine with the upper spine fixed.

(a). Lying on the back.
Knees bent. "Hollow" the lower back—(hyper-extension)—press it down against the floor (flexion).

(b). Repeat with knees straight as possible.
Explain.

Upper Part of Body—Cont.

(c). Knee-head position.

The upper back is more or less fixed because the head is on the floor.

(Other combinations for the various parts of the spine may be evolved from these few suggestions.)

It is well at this point to explain the advantage of working for elevation in the thoracic spine rather than for hyper-extension of the lumbar spine. The extreme backward bending and back-ward kicking which is so often taught and even sought after by the unen-lightened not only is likely to prove in-jurious but is offensive to artistic move-ment. Height is not necessarily increased by such action; indeed, it is naturally shortened. This fact can be demon-strated in the following manner:

Have one of the pupils lie on the floor on her side in a flexed position, with both feet against the wall. Ask her to push herself away from the wall, stretching to her full length, but bending back as far as she can from .the waist. Mark on the floor the point reached by her head. Notice the distance from the wall to this point, and its relation to the feet. Repeat the exercise, but instead of taking the backward bend at the waist, let extension pass through it, as it were, and carry the

Upper Part of Body—Cont.

chest high; that is, take complete extension in the thoracic and cervical
spine. Measure as before and notice the
distance. This does not mean that the
control of the lumbar spine should block
the movement there and hold it inactive
—this would result in limited and stiff
back movements. What it means is that
this control of the lumbar spine should
produce that flexibility which its position
and relations to the rest of the body make
so essential to true and plastic movement.

B. Lateral Movement.

a. Sitting on floor or in chair bend from one side
to the other, noting how free the movement
is in the neck and more limited in the lumbar
region. Repeat with body bent forward, and
with feet in side-stride position permitting
more movement in the lumbar spine.

b. Lying on the back with legs extended and
held down. Bend sideward as far as possible
letting head, shoulder and arms drag. Change
position of arms (overhead, shoulder high,
down at sides).

c. Lying on face, with body slightly elevated.

d. Standing on toes with heels back against the
wall.

C. Rotation, sitting on stool or on floor.

a. Twist trunk, turning head around as far as
possible.

b. Same with localization in different regions.

Upper Part of Body—Cont.

    c. Experiment standing up.

        (1). With hips fixed,

        (2). With hips free but ankles fixed,

        (3). With ankles and hips free.

        These exercises show how limited rotation is in the spine alone, that the range of this movement depends upon the rotation of the pelvis on the thighs, and the freedom of the ankles.

    d. As in rolls, which will be taken up later.

D. Circumduction.

Explain how circumduction is a combination of flexion, extension, rotation, and lateral bending. Take with different leads and try for wide, rangy, free, and complete movement.

    a. Sitting.

    b. Half kneeling.

    c. Kneeling.

    d. Standing.

    e. Lying across stool with partner holding feet. (Very strenuous.)

  2. MOVEMENTS OF THE UPPER LIMBS AND THE SHOULDER GIRDLE.

A review of the structure of the arms and their connection with the trunk reveals that the shoulder girdle and arms are particularly well adapted for freedom of movement. In the skeleton the upper limbs are indirectly connected to the spine by means of the shoulder girdle, which is composed in front on either side of two bones, the collar-bones or clavicles,

Upper Part of Body—Cont.

and in back on either side, of two bones, the shoulder blades or scapulæ. The collar bones articulate with the upper end of the sternum or breast bone of the thorax. It is this joint that forms the only connection with the skeleton of the trunk. The shoulder blades are only indirectly connected with the spine, and that is through their connection with the collar bones. Although in the actual skeletal construction the scapulæ are not directly connected with the spine, they are closely connected with the trunk because of muscular connections. Because of the combination movements made possible by the structure of the girdle and the fact that the scapulæ are not articulated with the thorax, there results a large range of movement in the girdle as a whole. It will be noticed, too, that the upper arm also articulates with the scapulæ at the shoulder joint. Because of this close connection between the upper limbs, the shoulder girdle and the trunk, in structure and muscle arrangement, it can readily be seen how movement in one part will affect or be affected by movement of another part. If the student is clear as to the structure of the shoulder girdle, and the close relation that exists between its movements and those of the arms and trunk, it will be much easier for him to master the control of the arms. A great deal of otherwise beautiful dancing is spoiled by stiff and angular arms. The amateur dancer does not usually realize that the arms are not a separate entity but are attached to the shoulder girdle, and that there is interaction of the muscle groups of arm,

Upper Part of Body—Cont.

shoulder, and trunk. The movements of the different parts of the arm and hand may of course be localized and taken independently of each other, and of the shoulder and back; often such localized movements are needed for expressive purposes as in some character dances and pantomime. But on the whole, arm movements are freer, more graceful and expressive when coördinated with those of the shoulder or back, or both, according to the movement desired.

A. Movements of the Shoulder Girdle.

(To avoid repetition of direction take the exercises in the following order—from one side to the other, alternate, then both together.)

Before starting the class on an analytical study of shoulder movements, have them sit on the floor, tailor fashion, with hands resting on the knees—later with elbows at sides which helps to localize the movement. Let them experiment and discover movements for themselves. Encourage them to take as large and as free movements as possible and in all possible directions. A student who is having difficulty in "finding" movement can be easily helped if the instructor will take hold of her shoulders and produce the action for her. After the students have become acquainted with the shoulder action, analyze the simple movements of which the more complicated movements are composed.

Since the movements of the shoulder girdle are the combined movements of its parts, it will be

Upper Part of Body—Cont.

more convenient for our purposes to resolve these movements into the movements of the scapulæ. Movements common to the scapulæ are: 1. Depression—pulling the shoulder down; 2. Elevation—raising or shrugging the shoulder; 3. Adduction—drawing the scapulæ closer to the spine, which pulls the shoulders back; 4. Abduction—as in pushing forward, which draws the shoulder forward, also as in forward and drooping shoulders; 5. Rotation—occuring when arms are raised higher than shoulder level; 6. Circling or circumduction.

Take the movements in the following positions.

a. Lying on the face.

(1). Arms at side. Palms up, palms down.

(2). Arms shoulder high. Same.

(3). Arms overhead. Explain as the arm is carried higher than shoulder level that the movement is not in the shoulder joint but is made possible by the rotation of the scapulæ. Same.

b. Lying on back.

Same series.

(1). With knees bent, to avoid hyper-extension in lumbar spine, especially in adduction and depression of the scapulæ.

(2). With knees straight if lower back can be controlled.

c. Sitting up with head forward on one knee flexed—a position which by fixing the spine, isolates the shoulders and aids localization.

Upper Part of Body—Cont.

   (1). With arms hanging at side. Same series.
   (2). With arm weight supported on the
        shoulders to bring in the element of
        gravity, which makes the movement more
        difficult and complex. Same series.
B. Movements of the Arm.
   The term arm is used to indicate the whole upper
   limb, *i. e.* upper arm, lower arm, and hand.
   a. Upper Arm.
   The upper arm articulates with the shoulder
   girdle at the shoulder joint—a ball and socket
   joint which permits of a wide range of movement. The result is that movement in the
   shoulder joint may take place in every direction. The movements of the upper arm will
   be spoken of in terms of the movement in the
   shoulder joint.
   (1). Flexion, moving the arm forward. In
        complete flexion movement is completed
        by the rotation of the scapulæ.
   (2). Extension, moving the arm backward.
   (3). Abduction, raising the arm from the side.
        If carried to overhead position, the action
        is not in the shoulder joint but in the
        rotation of scapula.
   (4). Adduction, bringing the arm down to the
        side or carrying it across the body in back
        or front.
   (5). Rotation, turning the arm on its long axis.
   (6). Circumduction, a combination of 1, 2, 3,
        and 4 in which the arm describes a cone.

Upper Part of Body—Cont.

b. Forearm.

The forearm consists of two bones freely movable on one another. Have the class experiment first by holding the arm with the palms up and noticing that the bones in this position are side by side, then by turning the palms down and noticing that the bones are in such a position that the outer bone is the inner bone. The two movements are:

(1). Supination, whereby the palm is turned upward.

(2). Pronation, the opposite movement whereby the palm is turned down.

c. The elbow joint.

The elbow joint is a hinge type of joint which articulates the forearm with the upper arm. The typical movements at this joint are:

(1). Flexion—which causes the forearm to be bent upon the upper arm.

(2). Extension—which straightens the forearm to practically a straight line with the upper arm.

The movements of the forearm may be executed in the different planes according to the position of the upper arm.

d. Hand.

A sensitive, well-developed hand is essential as the finish of well controlled and coördinated arm movements. Although the hands are almost in constant activity carrying out ideas and serving us, it is in a utilitarian

Upper Part of Body—Cont.

manner; so when we free them of objective use and try to use them for self-expressive purposes with arm movements, they prove to be a problem—they are stiff and inarticulate. The hand is a characteristic feature of man and, as is well known, may become a most sensitive and capable medium of expression. A study of the hand reveals a mobile and delicate structure. Its development depends on rendering it sensitive to movement, which may be done by exercising it in all possible ways—such as clenching the fists in different ways; spreading the palm; flexion and extension, abduction and adduction of the fingers; and combining these movements with those of the wrist, *i. e.* flexion, extension, side to side movement (abduction and adduction), and circumduction. The twisting movement of the hand has already been referred to as being caused by the crossing of the bones of the forearm.

C. Coördination of the Whole Arm.

The movements of the arm have been analyzed into the simple movements of its parts. It is a question now of coördinating these separate moving parts into a series of movements. Because of the close association between the shoulder girdle and arm already alluded to, there is not much of value that can be executed independently. However, it is advisable to work for flexion and extension and rotation in a well

Upper Part of Body—Cont.

coördinated series extending throughout the arm before associating these movements with those of the shoulder girdle. At first exercise the arms in a hanging position, which relieves them of working against the force of gravity. After the degree of mobility within the arm is determined and controlled, progress by gradually raising the arm only so high as not to involve a change of position in the scapulæ. Vary this exercise by taking in the different planes.

D. Coördination of Shoulder Girdle and Arm.

Up to this point the movements of the shoulder girdle and arm have been separate. The next step in progression is to coördinate their movements. It may be helpful now to think of the arm as being lengthened by the addition of the shoulder girdle, and being moved by movement starting in the shoulder. The control is seriously complicated by the arms becoming a load on the shoulder. A helpful way of beginning this study is to have the students stand and lean forward, with arms dangling. In this position they are not supported by the back and shoulder against gravity. In this position, have the class take free and large shoulder movements, and point out the action of the arms when allowed to dangle, and when stiffened. Continue this exercise, gradually raising the trunk and extending the arms well overhead. With untrained workers it will be noticed that the arms gradually stiffen as they reach a position of full extension.

Upper Part of Body—Cont.

This preliminary work affords an interesting example of the difficulty of this type of arm control and offers an opportunity to explain the mechanics of this type of leverage as applied to the shoulder-arm mechanism. Since we are not yet considering combined movements with the spine, it will be noted that the positions taken by the body are such as to isolate the shoulder. We are still concerned with localized control. Therefore, positions must be suggested that are favorable to this aim.

It will be clear that the first step in working out a series of exercises for coördinating shoulders and arms—those will come first that have to do with the movements of the shoulder carrying the arms merely as a load—is to hold the arm stiff as if it were a rigid unit, then gradually relax it, aiming for coördination with the shoulder and a flowing movement of the whole arm. Usually when the student is initiated into this problem, he will be very conscious of his hands. It has proved helpful to approach finished arm and hand work by considering the exercise as a test of the power of accurate discrimination of the student's kinesthetic sense, to see if he can tell by the report to his consciousness of the moving muscles and joints if all parts of shoulder, arm, and hands have been included in the exercise. This is a point that should often be brought to the attention of the student during that phase of our study that is helping him to discover his

Upper Part of Body—Cont.

own nature and overcome the inhibitions which are obstacles to his freedom of control. Gradually, the exercises become modified by the sense of their own effect, until the student gains such a mastery as will enable him to use them intentionally for their values when he is building the dance.

At first the exercises are done with the arm held in the one position, then with the arm carried through space, varying the movements by changing the planes and the height in which the arm is held.

Since all the exercises of this part are dependent upon the movements possible in the shoulder girdle, it will save needless repetition if those movements are referred to and used in combinations with the arms.

A few further suggestions are added.

a. Lying on the floor.

(1). Abduction and adduction.

(a). Face down, with arms overhead and lying on the floor.

(*1*). Backs of hands together. *Pull* (not lower) arms down to the sides letting them be dragged along the floor. Relax.

(*2*). Palms facing. Same. Call attention to the difference in difficulty made by the simple change of the position of the hands.

Upper Part of Body—Cont.

> (b). On the Back.
>> (*1*). Same as above. Take first with bent knees, feet on the floor; then with legs extended as far as possible without losing control of the lower back.
>> Call attention to the tendency of the lower back to hollow, as the effort is made to depress the scapulae. Explain the interaction of the back muscles, especially that of the latissimus. Use chart or skeleton. This position is one that enables the student to experience the difficulty of control of the lower back in those exercises that involve depression of the scapulæ; at the same time the position is one in which it is easy for him to control the lumbar spine by pressing it against the floor.
>> (*2*). Cross the arms in front. Carry arms out to side.
> (2). Flexion and extension.
>> (a). Forward upward and forward downward pulling of arms. Take with knees bent, lumbar back pressed against floor. Repeat with legs extended.

*Upper Part of Body—*Cont.

Control lumbar spine.

Distinguish between starting the movement in the shoulder girdle and permitting the arm to follow this lead, and starting the movement in the arm, in which case the shoulder girdle is affected by the arm lead.

Explain.

(b). Flexion and extension of arms in the lateral plane. Arms relaxed on the floor at shoulder level. Knees bent and lower back against floor. Bring back of the hands together over the head by starting the pull in the shoulders (adduction) and permitting the elbows to bend. (Keep arms always on the floor). With the backs of hands together stretch arms, hands and fingers to complete extension, starting the movement by a "Pushing-up" from the shoulders. Abduct, or spread arms to shoulder level. Suggest large movements.

b. Sitting up. Rest head forward on flexed knee. This position fixes the spine, leaving the shoulder girdle and arms free for localized movement.

Use any of the exercises that have already been suggested for the shoulder and arms,

Upper Part of Body—Cont.

    making combinations that are suggested from an understanding of their respective movements.

  c. Repeat any of the above with the body in the position of the crawl (See Plate XIII, Fig. 1, page 252). The balance is difficult because it requires excellent control not to stiffen and brace in the arms. The various shoulder and arm exercises taken in this position are an interesting test of control.

    For example—start with arm at side on floor; lift it backward and upward, carrying it to position overhead. Reverse and carry arm back and down to starting position. Take with both arms.

  d. Sitting up.
    Same.

  e. Standing up.
    Same.

    (Take with chest expansion and contraction combined with breathing.)

  f. Take inverted movement, that is, pulling the arms in toward the body. Take with varying degrees of energy. Since the emphasis is on flexion, the relaxation is taken with extension.

3. EXERCISES COÖRDINATING SPINE, SHOULDER GIRDLE AND ARM.

In this category of our study we are considering all movement that is possible in the upper part of the body. One has but to reflect upon his own be-

Upper Part of Body—Cont.

havior to realize the wide and varied range of action of which he is capable. As we depart from the mechanical and organic consideration of the elements of movement and mass them into larger and more inclusive movements, we are approaching that phase of our study that carries us from the mechanical determining of movements to that more important determining factor—the psychological. The study of anatomy, physics, and kinesiology tells us what movements we might be able to make because of our structure, but fails to explain those sensations and feelings back of our movements that determine our behavior. Since in these we are dealing with personalities as well as bodies, it is important that we be familiar with the laws of human behavior and response, that we understand the progressive forces at work in each individual, and know how to bring about a coöperation with them. These laws must be studied and known so that each individual may learn to be guided by them. It is in these exercises that include more and more parts coöperating together that we can begin to study meaning and feeling. It also is in this phase of our study that self-consciousness is most likely to appear. Consequently, the greatest care must be practiced with beginners when working for emotional response. It is better to spend more time on the study of movement as such until self-consciousness is mastered. Experience has led the writer to believe sincerely in the solution of the problem of self-consciousness, through the study of movement in the manner set

Upper Part of Body—Cont.

forth, *i. e.* by giving the student knowledge and understanding of what he is doing. As he gains mastery through conscious control, he becomes more and more absorbed in what he is doing and less and less concerned about the self that is doing it. Only when self-consciousness is overcome, can there be that spontaniety which follows purely internal suggestion regardless of all external interference. We may then distinguish between mechanical and expressive movements, but we cannot separate them. Behind the excitations of our muscles there are sensations and feelings and emotions which are the psychological determination of our actions, but these actions, as we have seen, are of necessity closely connected with the mechanical factors of our joint mechanism. Therefore, our task is to work for a higher beauty of movement through a mechanical beauty. We are concerned in suffusing body mechanics with that feeling and spirit which gives it true grace—a fusing of emotional and mental with the physical. Enough has been said to make the instructor realize her responsibility in dealing with plastic human bodies, minds and emotions. Because of existing individual differences she must be able to approach them and present her subject in many different ways and from many different angles, so that it will become of vital importance to each member in the class.

Since the movements of the trunk are determined by the action of the spine, it will be more convenient to group the headings in reference to its movements.

Upper Part of Body—Cont.

The exercises may be varied by changing the point of application of effort. For example, we may start the particular movement in the shoulder, in which case the movement that takes place in the spine and arms is determined by the direction of the force applied in the shoulder; or we may start movement in one of the regions of the spine, in which case the shoulder and arm obey the impulses so initiated. The exercises, then, that include the coördination of the upper part of the body are simply the combination of those simple movements of its parts. It would make too confusing an outline to attempt to include all the possible combinations, but if the principle of invention is clearly understood, there is no end of interesting movements that can be developed. It is always well to keep challenging the students to test their own kinesthetic sense. It helps to relieve self-consciousness and leads them into fresh modification of their work from thus sensing its effect. All that is necessary to suggest here is that they turn back to the spine exercises and include those of the shoulder and arm. All the exercises may be varied by taking different leads, changing the accent and intensity of effort. The difficulty of an exercise is increased by changes in the base of support and the height that it is executed from the floor; also by more complicated arm positions and combinations. The progression of bases is usually from lying to sitting on the floor tailor fashion, sitting on the heels, kneeling, half-kneeling to standing on the feet, and finally, standing on the

Upper Part of Body—Cont.

toes. The standing base is also affected in turn by the width of its base.

A. Flexion and Extension.

Here too, the building of the exercises depends on combining the various movements of the parts concerned. Variety depends on the same elements of invention as have already been mentioned. A few positions are added.

a. Sitting on edge of stool, extend the free leg back with instep on the floor. If necessary grasp the stool with the hand of the side that is on the stool. At all times work for a complete range of movement and a feeling of "follow-through." Raise body out of hips. Guard against excessive hyper-extension.

b. Sitting on a chair.

As in I, 1, A, b (b), p. 69 .

Add arm movement, changing leads and intensity.

B. Rotation.

a. As in the rolls—see Plates VIII, IX and X, pages 247, 248, and 249.

b. Half-lying position.

Weight supported on one arm and the lower body. Take as much rotation as possible within limits of position.

(1). With shoulder lead.

(2). With latissimus pull.

c. Standing with broad base.

Same as b, (1) and (2).

d. Carry over into locomotion.

Upper Part of Body—Cont.
  C. Lateral bending.
     With arm combination.
  D. Circumduction.
     Add arm combinations.
     Develop exercises as has already been suggested.
     Use scarf, held at end in one hand, or a scarf in
     each hand. They suggest large movement.

II. THE LOWER LIMBS.

That dancer is indeed handicapped who has not complete and effective control of the muscles of this part of the body. The feet especially must be sensitive and responsive to the music, whether it be light and quick, or strong and slow. The student also wants to be able to leap high and to leap vigorously when the occasion demands. In the study of the legs, the interest should be the development of strength, for the support of the body, and of agility, for the sake of the rhythmic vitality of the particular dance. Their action should always be in accord with the spirit of the dance. Too often spectacular leg work is indulged in at the expense of beauty and of harmonious body action.

The term "leg" is here used to include thigh, lower leg and foot. Explain the structure of the pelvic girdle by means of chart or skeleton, pointing out that movement in the girdle affects the parts attached—that the positions and actions of the thigh determine to a great extent those of the whole leg. Distinguish between movement in the leg independent of the lower back and that coördinated with it.

The Lower Limbs—Cont.

The movements may be taken in slow or quick, vigorous time. For slow time use a flowing 6/8 selection such as Schuman's "Slumber Song" or "The Palms," and some slow waltzes. For vigorous action use "Faust Waltz." Before considering the action of the legs, it may be well to refer again to the pelvic girdle, using a chart or skeleton, and review the structure of the pelvis. Discuss how the legs are connected with the upper part only by means of the pelvic girdle which is immovable on the spine. The bones of the pelvis are united to form a strong support for the trunk through which the weight of the trunk is transferred to the legs. Make a comparison of the movements of the shoulder and hip joint. Because of the position and function of the girdle, point out the mechanical necessity of a firm immovable joint between it and the spinal column, and of a strong fixed base for the support of the rest of the movable parts of the spine. Point out also how the obliquity of the pelvis is affected by movement in the lumbar spine; also explain how the iliofemoral ligament prevents extension backward of the thigh.

Before starting with work for localized control, have the class experiment and discover what movement they can in their hips. This may be done lying on the floor, on one side, sitting on the edge of a stool with one hip free, and standing with weight on one foot, with or without support.

1. HIP, FOR LOCALIZED CONTROL.

Review pelvic control of Part I with reference to leg action. The development of the muscles of the hip and their control is essential to the support of

The Lower Limbs—Cont.

the body in difficult positions of balancing, especially in positions of extreme extension with weight on the toes. Their action is most important for the correction of faulty foot positions as well as for the control of the alignment of the whole leg.

A. Flexion and extension, lying on the floor.

   a. On the back, with feet evenly together. Slightly lift one foot and touch the floor as far ahead as possible, so that one leg seems longer than the other. Return to original position, and take other leg. Alternate and repeat. It is a pushing and a pulling with the hip.

   b. On the face. Same. Touching the toe instead of the heel.

B. Vigorous static construction of gluteal muscles. (It is not very likely that untrained students will "find" the control at first. It is often necessary for the instructor to help a student by taking hold of these muscles and gripping them as if they were contracting. Very soon control is found.)

   a. Sitting on the floor, legs extended, knees easy, arms in back leaning rest position.

     (1). Take with and without outward rotation.

     (2). Take with and without inward rotation.

     (3). Same without arm support.

   b. Kneeling or standing. Contraction of gluteal muscles. Note change in pelvic tilt due to the coöpera-

The Lower Limbs—Cont.

tive action of lower back and abdominal muscles.

c. On tiptoes with support for balance.

Take with varying degrees of force in different tempos.

2. THIGH.

It will be observed that many of the following exercises as a matter of course naturally include the action of the whole leg, and might well be given in that group of exercises, but since the movements of the leg are dependent upon those of the thigh, it may be well to include some of them here.

A. Rotation—outward and inward.

a. Sitting on the floor, legs extended, knees relaxed, arms in back leaning rest. Notice the effect on position of lower leg and foot.

Explain.

Take with and without resistance.

b. Standing.

(1). Weight on one foot, knee of free leg flexed so that the movement is localized more definitely.

(2). Same with free leg extended in front. Notice position of foot. Place foot of rotated leg on the floor, noticing the different kinds of bases that result.

Repeat with leg extended in back.

Discuss.

The Lower Limbs—Cont.

B. Flexion.

   a. Sitting on the floor.

      Legs forward—arms in back leaning rest position. Lift one leg off the floor, first with stiff knee, then with relaxed knee, and finally with "easy" knee, *i. e.* knee slightly relaxed.
Repeat with antagonistic contraction.
Explain the leverage and compare with the similar control of arms.

   b. Sitting on stool.

      Flex thigh with a partner offering resistance by bearing weight upon thigh. It suggests lifting a load, which helps to localize the lift.

   c. Standing, with weight on one foot.

      (1). Flex thigh forward with knee flexed, knee straight and knee easy. With and without static contraction of gluteal muscles.

      (2). Swing leg freely forward with knee easy and instep extended. Notice the range of movement. Repeat with knee straight and instep flexed. Note how movement is limited because of the action of the ham string muscles. The latter exercise is good for stretching this group of muscles.

      (3). Other exercises that may be suggested are—

         (a). Bend forward and touch the floor with the hands, keeping the knees straight, weight well forward, and

The Lower Limbs—Cont.

feet together. If it is impossible to touch the floor with feet together, separate them, and gradually increase the distance until the feet are together.

(b). "Squat position." Both hands on the floor, weight on toes, heels raised, knees turned out. With a hop straighten knees, bringing feet together, flat on the floor and as near the hands as possible.

(4). Swing the leg freely, forward and backward, letting the body be turned by the force and momentum of the swing.

Take turning forward and backward.

(5). Swing the leg forward, permitting the momentum of the swing to lift the body off the floor and carry it forward. Alternate legs, going forward and backward. It may be well at this point to distinguish between locomotion due to the force of swing of the free leg and that due to the action (extension) of the supporting leg. Both may be carried over into dance forms as "step-hop." Moving from the swing gives "step-hop" with swing and movement forward rather than upward. When "step-hop" results from the extension of the supporting leg, there is more of a lift, and the body is carried higher. With the free leg passive there

The Lower Limbs—Cont.

is opportunity to vary the step by carrying the free leg forward with flexed or "easy" knee, and by carrying it extended. Take in different tempos and time, and have class decide which is the better adapted to the particular movement for the amount of effort expended. For examples: slow waltz, vigorous waltz— 2/4 and 4/4; slow 6/8 and quick 6/8.

C. Raising thigh backward.

Make clear that the action of raising the thigh backward takes place in lumbar spine. Experiment with the position taken by the leg when swinging backward and forward with a free pendular swing. Notice the outward rotation when swung backward without control of the alignment of the leg. Work for straight alignment—no rotation. It is always of interest to experiment further in this connection by having the free or extended leg assume its various positions on the floor, explaining the balance of the body, and showing how its alignment is affected by its base, and the relative position of the foot, whether the weight is supported on one or both feet. In trying these positions it is readily seen that the outward rotated and flexed knee of the leg extended backward gives at once a comedy base. Do not work for exaggerated positions; they are not apt to be refined, and they are very likely to cause strain in the lower back.

a. Lying on face, with one knee flexed (to aid

The Lower Limbs—Cont.

localization and to shorten the leverage), other leg extended.

   (1). Raise the thigh of flexed leg off the floor. Watch the alignment and avoid extreme hyper-extension in the lumbar spine. Movement is limited when taken without outward rotation. Explain.

   (2). Repeat with leg straight, knee tense; knee easy. It is helpful for the instructor or partner to hold legs in position to enable the student to sense the correct position.

   b. Crawl position.

   (1). Raise extended leg—knee easy. Movement is very slight because of the flexed position of the lumbar spine. Explain. This is an excellent exercise for localization.

   c. Standing, with and without support, and weight on one foot.

   (1). With knee flexed.

   (2). With knee extended but easy.

   d. Standing on toes. Same.

   D. Abduction and adduction.

   a. Sitting on the floor.

   (1). Separate feet away from the median line of the body—abduction. Return to position toward the body—adduction. Alternate and take both together.

The Lower Limbs—Cont.

        (2). From feet together, cross one leg over the other—adduction.

        Same from abduction position.

    b. Standing.

        (1) Jump with feet apart—sideways. Together.

        (2). Jump with feet across each other. Alternate the crossing.

        (3). Jump off the floor crossing them as many times as possible before landing.

        (4). Same—only striking feet.

        (5). Hopping on one foot.

            (a). Touch toe of other foot at the side, in front, in back, across in front, across in back. Same with heel. Alternate toe and heel. Make combinations and continue in series. Repeat on a moving base—hopping forward and backward, turning, and so on, in the different directions.

            (b). Cross right foot over the left and step, putting the weight on the right foot. Hop right and at the same time abduct the left (swing it to the side) and hit feet together while off the floor. Land on the right foot. Step across with the left;—hop and hit feet together. Continue.

            This exercise also may be done by hitting feet in front moving forward, also in back, moving backward. In

The Lower Limbs—Cont.

this do flexion and extension, not abduction and adduction.

E. Circumduction.

Standing.

With knee flexed, and with knee extended. With and without support.

F. "Reaching" with knee.

    a. Sitting on stool or chair, both hands clasping side of stool for support. Weight on one side, knee of exercised leg flexed. Reach forward as far as possible with the knee of flexed leg.

    b. Standing. Same.

    This is a very good exercise for developing localization and coördination in lower back and hip. Explain the action in the hip of supporting leg.

3. LOWER LEG.

Flexion and extension of knee only. Explain. May be taken in the different planes according to the position of the thigh.

4. FOOT.

The development of the foot is very essential to the development of balance. All sensation of change of equilibrium is registered in the feet, and only when they are strong and flexible are they capable of responding to a rapidly changing center of gravity. It is never safe to permit the class to engage in vigorous leaps and hops or aërial turns until the legs

The Lower Limbs—Cont.

and especially the feet have had the necessary development to insure correct landings. Transverse arches may fall under the strain, or injuries may result in other parts because of falls. Explain the series of arches that go to make up the structure of the foot, showing how they give strength combined with elasticity of movement.

At first experiment in the standing position. Explain the transference of the body weight through the legs to the feet. Have each student discover where his own weight line passes through his foot by following the finger in an imaginary line from the knee down the shin bone, on thru the foot, to a point somewhere between the great toe and the neighboring one. Assume different standing positions by changing the weight, throw it on the outside—on the inside, back on the heels, over the middle part, on the ball and toes, further forward on the toes with the ball of the foot off the floor, and finally with the weight correctly placed for a good standing position—heels lightly touching, toes straight ahead, and the weight forward at the point cut by the weight line. Repeat the foot positions on wide and small bases—all of which reveal the importance of strength of limb and feet for maintaining the sure and accurate base which is so essential to poise. Although we are still placing emphasis on the movements of the various parts, it will be appreciated that in those exercises taken in the standing position wherein the feet are raised from the floor, there will of necessity be movement in the whole leg.

The Lower Limbs—Cont.

A. Sitting on the floor.

With legs extended move the foot in all possible directions in free experimentation;—then explain the alignment in the different positions (flexion, extension, circumduction, eversion, inversion) especially in flexion and extension of the instep with and without an equilateral pull. Flex and extend toes. Have students watch the action of their feet.

B. On one knee and foot.

Place the foot of the forward leg firmly on the floor, pointing straight ahead. To make the position more comfortable rest the arm on the forward knee. As before, have students watch their feet. Repeat the transferring of the weight to different parts of the foot with the whole foot on the floor. Reduce the base by gradually raising the heel until there is complete extension in the instep, and the weight is well forward on the toes, with the ball lifted off the floor. Avoid inversion; keep the alignment straight. Repeat, letting the heel touch first, with the ankle well flexed, as the whole foot returns to the floor. Take the transference forward from heel through toes in smooth and complete sequence. Reverse the action, transferring the weight through the foot from tiptoe to heel. (Knee pads should be used for the supporting knee.) If chairs are available, the above exercise may be done sitting on them—in which case the exercises could be varied by

The Lower Limbs—Cont.

alternating the feet and then taking them together.

C. Standing.

Repeat the same with the body weight on the feet. Transfer weight from heel through foot to toes. Alternate from one foot to the other. Strive for complete extension of the ankle and an equilateral pull.

This is the action of the foot in walking, but of course with less extension of the ankle. Take same with complete flexion of the toes. The latter is an excellent exercise for the transverse arch—but should not be encouraged for use in the dance as it makes the foot look very drawn and tense.

a. Take heels raising and sinking. Until the class has good balance this exercise should be taken with some support—a chair, or the wall, or a partner. Gradually lift the heels higher. until weight is transferred forward on the toes.

b. Transfer weight from tiptoe to heel. Alternate from one foot to the other, which gives a pedaling motion. If balance is not good, use support. Keep the weight line true. In most running, leaping, hopping, skipping on the toes, also in moving backwards, it is the ball and toes that should receive the weight to make a light and safe landing.

c. Carry over into locomotion which is more difficult because the element of balance in locomotion is added.

The Lower Limbs—Cont.

5. EXERCISES COÖRDINATING THIGH, LOWER LEG, AND FOOT.

These exercises are merely the combining of the separately considered actions of the three parts. The aim here should be to combine into a smoothly working unit, with no muscular actions working against each other. Work for lower back control in all those exercises that involve the lumbar spine.

A. Flexion and extension.

   a. Lying on the back.

      (1). Knees bent, with feet on the floor, drawn up near the body. Further flex one leg by bringing knee to chest—extend and slowly lower extended leg to floor. Change legs and repeat. Take with both legs slowly sinking.

      This is good for toning abdominal muscles. Control lower back. Change by flexing trunk on thighs from lying on back position to sitting up. If necessary, feet should be held down. Progress in difficulty by gradually changing the length of the leverage. Take first with arms down at side, then with arms at side shoulder level, and finally with arms extended over head.

      (2). Same. Take flexion and extension of free leg as in (1), only on extension lift lower back off the floor, reaching high with the extended leg, raising the body up

The Lower Limbs—Cont.

on the shoulders and the toes of the supporting foot.

b. Lying on one side.

If lying on left side, completely flex right leg, extend as before, and carry it around and back as far as possible, keeping the foot on the floor. This avoids what would be a wide base if taken in the upright or standing position. Avoid stiff knee. Change sides.

c. Standing.

(1). On both feet. Review the action and support of the foot.

(a). Flexion and extension of thigh, leg and foot, with foot held in extension. Work in groups of threes—one student is the subject who uses the second to balance him while the third supports his heels which are raised as high as possible. The weight is well forward on the toes. The worker bends knees, then takes complete extension of whole leg. Do not let weight go to outside of feet. Feet should be close together and weight line should be maintained throughout the exercise. Take with pelvic control and strong static contraction of hip muscles.

(b). Repeat without heel support.

(c). Flexion and extension with transference of weight through the foot.

The Lower Limbs—Cont.

With weight on both feet, flex hips and knees. Then as legs take extension, pass the weight through the foot and rise on toes with complete extension. Take flexion again, letting heels come down, and on extension of legs, shift weight back on heels, lifting front part of foot off the floor with as much flexion in the ankle as possible.

Use chair or a partner for support. Carry over into a rocking movement. Take without support.

(2). Standing on one foot.

(a). Flex the other leg, extend, and lower. Take in different planes.

(b). Raise knee forward; lower and raise in back, permitting the body to bend forward in order that the alignment of the leg and foot may be seen. Avoid any outward rotation.

(c). Swing leg forward, knee easy and alignment correct, permitting the other knee to bend.

(d). Same, only rising on toes of the supporting foot as free leg is raised forward.

(e). Swing relaxed leg forward and backward like a pendulum and notice its tendency to outward rotation. Take with control.

The Lower Limbs—Cont.

(f). Have class, numbered off by 1's and 2's, work in circle with hands joined. When No. 1's work No. 2's serve for support, and vice versa.

Weight well balanced on toes of supporting foot, free leg raised forward; no rotation. Slow leg flexion; avoid letting knee of supporting leg turn out. Slow extension. Alternate legs.

(g). Sit on heel of flexed and supporting leg, with other leg extended at side, and heel on floor. Quickly change position of feet, and repeat.

Try without support, raising extended foot off ground.

(h). Same, only extending leg forward instead of sideways.

(i). "Running start" position.

Both hands on the floor, with body leaning well forward with weight over the supporting foot, and the other leg extended in back. Head should hang low enough for the student to observe the extended leg without difficulty. Raise the free leg off the floor as far as possible. (The position of the back, with head low and other hip flexed prevents any extreme extension in the lumbar spine. The relation of the free leg

The Lower Limbs—Cont.

to the body is the same as in standing.) Take with leg rotated out and in, and with flexed and extended knee. Finally, take with leg well balanced and controlled, knee easy, and the foot in true alignment with the rest of the leg. Explain the difference. By watching their movements, the students are enabled to find control more quickly. They are learning through sight as well as through feeling so that they are able to make corrections more intelligently. For this reason mirrors are of advantage.

Take without watching the positions, and see if the students can trust their kinesthetic sense to take correct positions.

d. Sitting on stool.

(1). Come to standing position on both feet. Experiment by changing position of feet.

(2). Come to standing position on one foot. Slowly rise and slowly sit down.

e. Standing on stool.

(If chair is used, it should be steadied.)

(1). One leg hanging free over the edge. Take free pendular swing. Notice the outward rotation and the tendency of knee to bend. Repeat with lower back and hip control. Check the swing at

The Lower Limbs—Cont.

different points to test the resultant positions.

(2). One foot on stool other on floor.

(a). Shift the weight forward through both feet until heels are well raised. Sink back on heels and repeat each time gathering more "sweep" and energy until the body is swung up and off the stool by a strong push-off with the leg on the floor. As the body comes down, the feet assume the same position, i. e. one foot on the stool and the other on the floor.

(b). Shift the body weight forward and over the leg on the stool. Slowly push the body up by extension of the supporting leg, carry the free leg with it. Avoid outward rotation in the free leg. This exercise is similar to No. (1) only the emphasis is on the extension of the leg on the stool instead of the leg on the floor.

f. Standing on head and shoulders, with legs extended in the air in the perpendicular plane. For the first few times the students will not be able to tell when their legs are perpendicular. The student can be helped to find the "feel" of the position if the instructor or a partner will put his hands where the feet of the subject should be. Have him touch the hand and assume the correct position until

The Lower Limbs—Cont.

he has found his balance and control. In this position the students are able to watch their legs in action and make corrections. The following exercises should not be given until backs are ready for it.

(1). With both legs extended and in good balance, reach high with feet, which means a stretching or extension in the spine. Keep straight alignment in legs.

(2). Flexion and extension of whole leg with wide range of movement. "Bicycle movement."

(3). Same movement only much refined. Take with as little action as possible without stiffening the leg. Have the movement start in the hip and progress through thigh, leg and foot. It "pulsates" through. This control is similar to the control of arm movement and demands excellent coördination.

(4). When backs are strong enough, take 1, 2, and 3 without hip support.

g. Carry coördination of leg over into locomotion. Control more difficult because the element of balance in the transference of weight is added.

(1). Walking. The most fundamental and common form of locomotion. The body never leaves the ground. In walking the weight of the body passes alternately from one leg to the other. The action

The Lower Limbs—Cont.

seems very simple, but when taken with correct balance and transference of weight, it is found to demand fine co-ordination. The chest should be held high, head easily poised, body lifted out of the hips, weight always forward and over the moving base. The weight is transferred from the heel through the foot at the point of intersection of the weight line. The foot points straight ahead.

(a). Slow time.

(1). One step to a measure of 4/4 time. "Chord grasps." Slow and continuous transference of weight from one foot to the other, and from heel to toe in each foot. Toe straight ahead. Try the effect of walking on the outside of the foot.

(2). Take 2 steps to the measure.

(b). Regular walk rhythm. 1 step to a beat. Any good march.

(1). Experiment by walking with knees stiff, body erect, which makes it easy for the student to avoid pounding with the heels. The quick transference from the heel to the forward part of the foot is not difficult when walking this way. Gradually relax

The Lower Limbs—Cont.

the knees and continue with the same foot work.

(2). Walk by transferring the weight in the following ways:

(a). Using the whole foot at once.

(b). Shortening the foot by raising the heel and transferring the weight from ball to toes.

(c). Raising the heel higher, lifting the ball off the floor, and walking on the bottom of toes only.

(d). Letting the toes and ball strike the floor first and the heel last.

(e). Letting the tips of the toe strike first, then the ball, then the heel.

(f). Walking as fast as possible without breaking into a run.

(g). A free normal walk, with the swing from the hips, body held out of hips, head up, and weight forward.

(h). Walk up and down stairs with the different movements of the feet. Discuss.

(i). Walk backwards and notice the action of the foot.

(c). Vary 1 (a) and 1 (b) by changing the

The Lower Limbs—Cont.

position of the body and arms. For example:

(1). With bent knees and body forward.

(2). Chest lifted high, head up and well back, arms extended forward.

(3). Same, with arm weight changed. Drop hands down on the head.

(4). Arms clasped in back, spine relaxed.

(5). Same, with lower and middle back extended, head hanging forward.

(6). Place both hands on left hip. Turn the right shoulder and head forward. Take in different tempos. Transfer weight from heel to toe. Let weight fall heavily upon the heels to contrast with the correct use of the foot.

(2). Running.

Is more rapid than walking, but as in walking, the steps follow each other at equal intervals. Since the body leaves the ground at each step, it is therefore more strenuous.

(a). Run using the whole foot with as little transference of weight through it as possible.

The Lower Limbs—Cont.

(b). Same, only transferring the weight through the foot from heel to toe.

(c). Run transferring the weight from toe to heel.

(d). Run on toes.

Take with different rates of speed.

(3). Leaping.

Is more strenuous than the run. The body is lifted higher off the floor. As in the walk and the run the steps follow at equal intervals and are continuous forms of progression.

The length of stride is greater.

Have the class take free leaping with only the idea of covering ground, or of getting height. Then take with control and co-ordination of back and arms.

(a). Leap with a good push off with the supporting leg. Take with extension of upper back, chest high. Carry over the control of the exercises of "reaching with the knee." After the extension of the supporting leg, let it trail.

(b). Leap with the "prancing step" (toe, heel).

(1). Letting the knees bend.

(2). With knees in front of body, feet on line with knee.

(3). With practically no action in the knees and the feet kept on a

The Lower Limbs—Cont.

line with the body or under the body. This is excellent leg exercise.

(4). Leap with low, long strides, and weight well forward.

(5). Leap with straight knees, and body bent low and forward; with body well back of moving base.

(4). Hopping.

(Landing on the same foot or on both feet.)

(a). Hop on both feet.

(b). Hop on one foot.

(c). Alternate.

(d). Make series.

Take in all directions.

(5). Skipping.

(Skipping may be considered as hopping in unequal intervals.)

(a). Skip with the whole foot, transferring from heel to toe.

(b). Skip on the toes.

Notice the effect of each.

Take in all directions in a series.

(6). Galloping.

(Galloping may be considered leaping in unequal time intervals.)

(a). With the right lead.

Right foot takes the strong accent and the left foot takes the weak accent.

The Lower Limbs—Cont.

(1). Forward—notice the right foot is ahead of the left.

(2). Backward—notice the right foot is back of the left.
These are the relative positions of the strong step to the weaker step which the legs naturally assume in the gallop.

(3). Repeat (1) but reverse the position of the feet, keeping the same lead, that is go forward but with the left foot (weak step) ahead of the right foot (the strong step).

(4). Repeat (2) with a reverse position of the feet that is go backward with right lead, but the right foot is ahead of the left.
(3) and (4) require good control and good sense of rhythm.

(5). Gallop sideward left with right foot crossing left in back.

(6). Gallop sideward left with right foot crossing left in front.

(7). Gallop sideward left alternating the crossing of feet.

(8). Gallop sideward right with left foot crossing right in front; in back.

(9). Gallop sideward right alternating the crossing of feet.

The Lower Limbs—Cont.

(10). Take in different directions.

(b). Repeat with the left lead.

(c). Combine (1) and (2) changing the lead.

(d). Take (1), (2), and (3) with flexed and straight leg.

(e). If steps are available, take (1), (2), (3), (4), (5), and (6) going up and down the steps. Is excellent practice for accurate foot work.

(7). Sliding.

Also executed in unequal time sequence. Is similar to the gallop in that it is a continuous form of locomotion. The gallop and slide differ in this respect from the skip, whose two parts, that is the "long-short" or "step-hop" is executed on one foot, then on the other. In the slide the feet slide on the floor, and when done slowly, is taken without the body quitting the floor. When it is taken vigorously, the body is lifted off the floor, but the action of the legs is the same, as when it is executed on the floor.

(a). Slide in all directions, changing the lead on different counts. For example: "Slide-slide-slide and change" is taken to 4/4 time, with one slide to each beat and "change" on the fourth.

"Slide and change," "slide and

The Lower Limbs—Cont.

change" is 2/4 time and carries over into the polka. When developed from the slide in this way, the polka may be taught in a very short time.

(8). Develop the waltz, schottische, polka, gavotte, and make new combinations, with the basic or alphabetical steps. All are only a matter of sequence or order of arrangement of the primary steps. For example, the schottische is a transference of weight in a "4-count" rhythm, using two steps, a dragging step and a hop in the order of "step, drag, step, hop." But if this order is rearranged and changed to "step-step-drag-hop" or again, to "hop-step-drag-step," we get a very different rhythmical sequence. Make combinations in two, three, four, and six count rhythm.

III. EXERCISES COÖRDINATING BACK AND LEGS.

These exercises are classified under the headings of the movements of the spine.

1. FLEXION AND EXTENSION.
   A. Lying on the floor.
      a. On one side. Flex back and legs bringing knee and head together. Take full extension of back and leg, carrying the leg as far as

Exercises Coördinating Back and Legs—Cont.

possible without extreme hyper-extension in
the lower back. Carry head and chest high
and well back. Vary the exercise by starting
extension in different parts of the body, head,
chest, hip, knee, foot.

b. Face down.

With strong extension of upper back, raise
leg off the floor only so far as it can be done
with good control.

Alternate legs. Take with both.

To avoid the body turning to one side in
raising one leg, keep both "hip bones" on the
floor as a guide.

c. On the back.

(1). Flex legs and back, touching feet on the
floor overhead, shifting the weight as far
up on the shoulders as possible. Slowly
let the back come down to the floor until
the whole spine touches the floor. Then
extend legs and take slow leg sinking,
controlling the lower back as the feet
approach the floor.

Take in slow and quick time.

(2). Alternate the feet, touching the floor
overhead.

If necessary support hips on hands.

B. On both hands and one knee.

Free leg held in good position in back.

Take flexion and extension of spine, noting the
effect on the pull of the raised leg.

Feel the lift in the upper back and chest.

Exercises Coördinating Back and Legs—Cont.

C. Preliminary Crawl.

Position as in Plate XIII, Fig. 1, page 252.

As the back comes up in extension, the weight is transferred on to the lower leg of flexed leg (instep on floor). The weight is gradually transferred forward on to the knee and the hands, which slide forward so as to broaden the base. As the body is carried forward, the free, or extended leg is raised and dragged forward with the instep on the floor. As the supporting leg becomes extended, the free leg flexes and reaches through hands as far as possible and receives the weight. Back is lowered in flexion to the original starting position. There is no transference of weight from one hand to the other (both support the body), only from one leg to the other. Vary the lead by starting extension in the lower middle and upper spine.

Take going backward.

D. "Reaching" with knee as in II F, page 99.

a. Forward.

Work in groups of three as it is best to have support on both sides.

Starting position is the body in full extension, well on the toes of supporting foot (right.) Head well back, chest high, other (left) leg is forward with knee flexed. Reach forward with left knee dragging the body after it. As it extends and the weight is transferred from the right foot to the left, the body falls back. After the left foot takes the weight, the body

Exercises Coördinating Back and Legs—Cont.

is brought forward in complete flexion, to compensate for the extension. Left leg also flexes. Adjust weight to correct part of the foot. Take complete extension of body and left leg and foot, bringing the right leg forward in flexion to the original starting position.

Repeat progressing forward.

b. Backward.

Starting position is with body flexed, but supporting right leg is extended and the left knee is flexed. Bring head and left knee together as nearly as possible. Extend left knee backward, coördinating it with extension of the spine. (Avoid excessive hyper-extension of lower spine and outward rotation of left leg).

Toes of back foot take the weight then it is transferred through the whole foot. Take complete flexion of the back, allowing left leg to bend also the right leg as it is flexed to the starting position. Aim to maintain correct alignment.

Repeat—progressing backward.

c. Take a and b without support. At first take in slow time. Music: "The Palms," or "Schmetterling." Then adjust the range of movement to a swinging waltz. Music.— Blue Danube Waltzes.

It is a good test of the student's powers of coördination and invention to explain the

Exercises Coördinating Back and Legs—Cont.

problems to them and let them solve them for themselves. For example, the problem may be the one just analyzed, that is, progressing forward and backward in the upright position with complete flexion and extension of spine and legs. It is assumed that they already have the mastery of the elements; it is now a question of putting them together and finding the answer. The problem set of course must include only those movements of which they are capable. Often interesting and original exercises result. The method challenges the student's interest and effort and stimulates them to inventive activity.

E. Sitting on heels, weight well forward on the toes, back completely flexed. Take complete extension of whole spine, and legs, keeping the weight well forward on the toes. (Heels will tend to lower as body weight is lifted higher.) Keep weight line correct. Take with good pelvic and lower back control. Slowly relax (flexion) to starting position.

F. Similar to E, only weight is on one foot with other leg raised in back. Avoid outward rotation. Raise heel of supporting foot, with body in partial flexion. Take extension of whole body with emphasis on getting the chest high (chest lead)— working for extreme extension in the upper back —and not in lower back. Take in slow time. The extended leg should now be considered as in extension of the spine. So, if upper part of spine

Exercises Coördinating Back and Legs—Cont.

is lifted, of necessity all that is attached to it will be raised. Thus the height of the free leg is affected by the action of the upper back. Distinguish between the free and extended leg being raised by flinging it back and being lifted by the extension of the upper back. Plenty of time should be given to the mastery of this control.

Take in quick time—putting all the emphasis and accent on the extension of upper spine.

G. Combine the chest lift with a moving base. For example "Slide and hold" lifting the chest on the "hold." Then take more vigorously and substitute a hop for the hold, lifting the body off the floor. "Slide and lift." Avoid flinging the free leg back and up. The aim is to coördinate the chest lift with the extension of the supporting leg. Music 3/4 Faust Waltz; 6/8 Sorrentina.

H. Standing with one foot on stool.
Weight forward.
Sweep up on stool with push off of supporting leg. Combine with chest lift. Avoid outward rotation of free leg, and extreme hyper-extension in lower spine. If necessary, have partner steady stool.

a. With body flexed forward over foot on stool.

(1). Take "heavy" lift, or pull up of the body coming to full extension of body and leg. Do not try to stand on toes until strength and balance are sufficiently developed. Control the free leg as in H. Slowly return to starting position.

Exercises Coördinating Back and Legs—Cont.

      (2). Repeat with the emphasis on the extension of the supporting leg. To explain, the leg "pushes" the body weight up.

      The body is a load on the leg.

      The first is a coördination of back and leg extension. In the latter, back extension follows leg extension. Avoid a "push off" with the free foot. Take with and without assistance.

I. Combine transference of weight from heel to toe and from one foot to the other with body flexion and extension. The result is a wave-like movement. The "pick-up" necessitates strong contraction of thigh extensors and abdominal muscles. Music; flowing 6/8 time—Slumber Song—*Schumann*.

2. ROTATION.

  A. Lying down.

    As in the first roll.

    Take with the lead in the leg and let the back follow. Let the various parts of the back lead and the legs follow.

  B. Standing.

    a. Weight on one foot. Take with support. Swing the leg across in back, letting the momentum of the swing lift the body up on the toes of the supporting foot. At the same time lift head and chest high—back free so as to be turned by the action of the leg.

Exercises Coördinating Back and Legs—Cont.

    b. Take without support. Swing leg forward and across making a complete turn.

    c. Repeat with the force of the swing lifting the body off the floor; progress with a "step-hop." Distinguish between turning with upper body leading, and the lower following, and the legs leading and the upper body following.

    Take both ways.

    Use smooth 6/8 or waltz rhythm at first.

    Later execute more vigorously, turning with a hop.

IV. EXERCISES WITH THE BODY MOVING AS A UNIT.

Up to this point our study has been to gain a knowledge and mastery of the body mechanism. The parts have been studied in their relation to each other and to the whole, and the possibility for a great variety of movements has been made clear. The next step is to consider the body moving as a coördinated whole.

All movements of the parts may now be combined. In the combinations work from the simple to the more complex, the relation of parts to the whole will differ in the various positions, but the intelligent worker will keep control at all times. The effect of the pull of gravity on the body in its different positions must also be taken into consideration. In carrying the movements over to a moving base care should be taken not to lose control of the various muscular centers. The teacher will be able to add to this list, since these exercises contain elements

Exercises with the Body Moving as a Unit—Cont.

of growth within themselves that suggest still others. Moreover, when the student has mastered all the technique possible in the "rolls," "folding and unfolding" and the "crawl," so that he is able to adjust to any change of lead and position, he is doing many things well. These fundamentals furnish a group of exercises which demand a control that is applicable to a wide variety of movement and that affords ample opportunity for much study and practice.

1. FLEXION AND EXTENSION.

All the exercises of Part III may be included in this section by adding arm movements.

A. Folding and unfolding. See Plates XI and XII, pages 250 and 251.

a. Horizontal plane.

(1). Lying on the floor, face down.

(a). Forward.

Adjust weight so that it is on the forearms, with the hands placed firmly on the floor, palms down. Lift the knees and bring them well up under the chest to a completely flexed position as in Fig. 1—Plate XI (Flexion or folding).

Stretch out until the whole body is extended. Movement progresses from knees, through hips, spine, shoulders, elbows, wrists, to fingers, (Extension or unfolding). Pads should be worn on the insteps to

Exercises with the Body Moving as a Unit—Cont.

prevent them from being rubbed as they are dragged along the floor. Repeat folding and unfolding, moving forward.

(b). Backward.

From full extension flex elbows at side, with fingers spread and hands placed firmly on the floor, palms down. Lift body up with weight on elbows and knees. Transfer weight back to the knees, flexing hips and knees. Body now sits back on heels; arms are dragged.

Flex arms as in Fig. 1., Plate XI (Flexion or folding). Take extension or unfolding by transferring the weight on to the elbows and forearms, and pushing the body back to full length. The movement now progresses from elbows through shoulders, spine, hips, knees to feet. Repeat flexion and extension, moving backward.

b. Vertical plane.

(1). Folding.

Start from the position of Fig. 6, Plate XII, but with weight forward on the foot instead of upon the toes. Start folding in the arms, by pulling them down with the upper back and shoulders. Do not take any flexion, or in this case,

Exercises with the Body Moving as a Unit—Cont.

relaxation, until the shoulders and arms have completely relaxed (given up to the pull of gravity). Then begin with the head and relax in the following order, neck, upper back, middle back, lower back, hips, knees, until the body is flexed as in Fig. 1, Plate XI. Notice that the insteps are on the floor. With beginners it is very difficult to maintain the proper balance as the positions of the various parts of the body change. For instance after the head drops forward, they are likely to continue movement by bending forward at the hips, at the same time permitting the weight to fall back on the heels and the knees to lock. This lack of balance and control is also observed in an adjustment that is commonly made by the arms. As the body is lowered or flexed, instead of the arms and shoulders remaining relaxed, and the arms dangling from the shoulders—which of course increases the difficulty of the balance since more weight is thrown forward—the arms are held at the side of the body. Then too the head is often raised as the body is flexed. These are positions that will need to be constantly watched for and corrected until the novice gains sufficient kinesthetic power to judge the sensations of movement

Exercises with the Body Moving as a Unit—Cont.

for himself. The surest way to maintain the proper poise is to keep the weight of the body forward on the foot at that point where the weight line passes through it. (The weight line is an imaginary line drawn from the knee, down the shin bone and the extended instep, on through the foot between the great toe and the adjacent one). Another common fault in the beginner's folding is that as the body approaches the floor near enough for the hands to touch, they take some of the weight and thereby broaden the base. When the folding is well done, the legs support the body and maintain balance with no help from the arms. At first the weight is evenly distributed on both feet. Later one side may be eased by raising the heel of one foot and placing the ball at the instep of the other foot. If necessary the knees may be held firmly together for support. Care must be taken not to "stand on one hip." There should be good pelvic and lower back control throughout. After the general principles of "giving up to gravity with control" or of "progressive relaxation" (folding) are understood, work for variation.

(a). Vary the leads and the degree of resistance of antagonistic muscles.

Exercises with the Body Moving as a Unit—Cont.

(b). Take with slow sinking on to the knees with the upper body well back for balance. Starting position should be in full extension with the weight on the toes—as in Fig. 6, Plate XII. If control is good and balance correctly adjusted, there should be no dropping on to the knee.

(c). Take flexion as the result of a sigh or exhaling of the breath, and then, as the reaction to a mood or idea suggested by the music. Note that wherever the movement is mechanically determined, it is executed in more or less the same manner, since all bodily mechanisms are similar. But wherever the movement springs out of feeling, individual differences will appear in the varying positions assumed by different bodies. It is only when the positions and movements of the body are associated with mental activity that they be come expressive of something more than mere mechanical skill of execution.

(2). Unfolding.
(Lifting the body against gravity).
Take position of Fig. 1, Plate XI.
Start the lift in the base of the back, lifting the hips as far as possible without

Exercises with the Body Moving as a Unit—Cont.

letting the head leave the floor. As the hips are lifted higher and the head comes up (but still hanging), one knee comes forward, and the foot takes the weight. The foot should be placed straight, and the weight should be forward. Continue lifting the hips; the trunk is now slowly lifted, or pushed up by the extension of the legs. Avoid pushing or supporting with the arms. Upper body is still relaxed and hanging heavy. Let the head and shoulders hang lower than the hips as long as possible. As the supporting leg is extended, the other foot is dragged up and the weight is evenly shifted to both feet. (Or to the ball of one foot as has been suggested). Extension goes through the whole spine, shoulders, arms, and fingers. When control and strength are sufficient, add the extension of the feet as in Fig. 6, Plate XII. Care should be taken to keep the weight forward and the lower back and pelvis controlled. (Aim for good posture.) Vary as in 1.

B. The Crawl. See plates XIII and XIV, pages 252–3. The crawl is very difficult because it demands strength, especially in the back, and a very high form of coördination.

Refer to the preliminary crawl, Part III, C, page 119. The completed crawl adds the coördination of shoulder and arm with transference of weight.

Exercises with the Body Moving as a Unit—Cont.

    a. Forward.

       (1). With arm and leg of same side.

       (2). With opposite arm and leg.

       (3). Without arms. Very difficult.

       Change the lead in the extension of the spine to the different parts.

    b. Backward.

       As in the preliminary crawl III, C, only with shoulder and arm combinations.

       In extension of spine change the lead to the different parts.

  C. Partners facing with hands joined:

    As one takes back extension, let the other follow with back flexion. Increase in difficulty by changing the base. Work from the whole foot to toe support. Shift support from the front to back leg with flexed and straight knees.

2. ROTATION.

  A. First Roll. See Plate VIII, page 247.

    At first have the class lie on the floor with arms overhead and roll any way. Then discuss with them the possibilities for control and coördination. The roll is the simplest and most satisfactory exercise for beginners to experience and study the laws of movement. After the class has rolled about informally for a sufficient length of time, have them take it with some order of effort and control.

    a. Lying on the back.

    Roll over on the face, starting the turn in the

Exercises with the Body Moving as a Unit—Cont.

hip (Suggest the movement by comparing it to a twisted rope). The hip leads, dragging the legs and upper body after it. The head should trail back as far as possible.

b. Lying on the face.

Movement starts in the upper back, head leading. Aim to get it as far ahead in the lead as possible with chest high.

c. Continue a and b; control abdominal and lower back muscles to avoid flopping. The body is carried over the floor with the work done by the back and abdominal muscles. After each turn add extension, or stretching of the whole body, sending it well through the arms and fingers and legs. This gives the sensation of the whole body completing the movement. When the roll in general is understood, begin to work for more localized control. Add the strong downward pull of the latissimus which gives the lead to the hip, and depresses the shoulder. Distinguish between the hip lead caused by this control, and that of (b), where the whole body is relaxed, without any active coördination of parts. At first, however, work for relaxed bodies, so that each part will be affected by the pull. In the beginning the movement should be flowing and the opposing muscles relaxed. Later use antagonistic contraction to offer resistance, but with care that no part of the body is tense. Notice the positions taken by the legs. When

Exercises with the Body Moving as a Unit—Cont.

the body is relaxed there is a flexion of the upper legs which broadens the base, thereby facilitating the balance. The roll is made more difficult by keeping knees straight and feet together, thus narrowing the base. When the roll is taken with the lead alternating from the lower back to the upper back, it gives a satisfying sequence of movement permitting the displacement of parts in their natural order. Change the sequence by varying the lead.

d. Roll with the lead kept in the hip. When on the face, the usual difficulty is that of keeping the movement following clear through the spine. At first the tendency will be to brace in the upper back. If backs are free and un-resisting there will be flexion, drawing the head and knees toward each other. In order that the movement may not be checked the instructor must keep reminding the students to watch constantly the impulse of movement that spreads from the center of the movement to the adjacent parts.

e. Roll with the lead kept in the upper back and the head. Try the chest lead which often proves helpful for more active extension in the thoracic spine.

f. Take with the arms lowered to the side, thus changing the distribution of the arm load. It is more difficult, but excellent for extension in the upper back, raising the chest high.

g. Change the order of the natural sequence of

Exercises with the Body Moving as a Unit—Cont.

parts. For example, when the hip leads from lying on the back, the order is hip, shoulder, head. Change to the following order—hip, head, shoulder.

h. Keep the lead in the shoulders. At first the tendency will be for the student to take the lead with the head which relieves the shoulder from dragging the full load. If the spine is relaxed, the shoulder pull causes the head to be flexed on the neck.

Take first in slow time, then with quick and vigorous action. Music:—"Faust Ballet Waltz." Keep the pull always in the shoulder. When this movement is taken in fast time, unless there is sufficient control, the tendency is to let the momentum of the movement carry the body.

This is an excellent exercise for freeing and developing shoulder and arm control. It should be carried over into the upright position where the shoulder pull directs the movement of the body on the feet, that is, the feet follow.

i. Vary the execution of the different ways of taking the roll, by checking the movement at different points, and holding the positions long enough to image kinesthetically the relative positions of all parts of the body. Then stand and take the same attitude in the upright position. This is an interesting and valuable way of getting the students into the

Exercises with the Body Moving as a Unit—Cont.

habit of making intelligent observations of their own sensations of movement and attitudes.

j. Take (a) and (b) with all the emphasis on lifting the chest high, an excellent preparation for taking the roll or "spiral turn" in the upright position with the combination of sliding and leaping. At first take with no attempt at setting a definite pattern or step for the feet. Let them be free to make any necessary and spontaneous adjustment for maintaining balance of the body, move in response to the "spiral" or rotation of the spine with emphasis on the chest lift. Later combine with a definite step, and as this becomes coördinated, add the turn with a leap.

B. Second Roll. See Plate IX, page 248.

The positions of the body in the second roll are more difficult than those of the first. This is because the size of the base is decreased and the upper part of the body supported off the floor. This means that muscular effort is expended to resist gravity. The control of this movement requires excellent shoulder and arm control. Abdominal strength and control are also essential. There should be mastery of the simple elements separately before they are coördinated into the more complex whole. When the body is in the position of Fig. 1, to avoid extreme hyper-extension in the lower back hold the abdomen off the floor by strong static contraction

Exercises with the Body Moving as a Unit—Cont.

of the abdominal, lower back, and hip muscles. Vary the leads as suggested in A.

C. Third Roll. See Plate X, page 249.

It is the most strenuous because it demands a great deal of strength and a fine degree of coördination. Vary the leads.

D. The "Spiral."

("Spiral" is a term used for the rolls executed in the upright position.)

a. Using the wall for support.

When the student first attempts to carry over the action of the body in the rolls to the standing position, he often has difficulty in orienting himself. It is helpful for him to face the wall, with arms overhead and hands touching (not leaning against) the wall. The head is also against the wall. Start the body turning around by swinging the one arm down and up to starting position, passing it between the body and the wall. The body has now twisted around so that the back is toward the the wall. Continue turning by swinging the other arm down and up, passing it between the wall and body as before. The head remains against the wall and pivots as the body twists around. This should be taken slowly so that the student can observe and study the positions his body goes through. Aim for a complete spiral as in the rolls. In the same position let the hands and head remain touching the wall and twist the body (observing

Exercises with the Body Moving as a Unit—Cont.

the path the hands take on the wall) with
attention given to the free action of the
shoulders. Repeat with only the hands against
the wall, and finally with the whole body free.

b. With partner.

Face partner and join both hands. Twist
under each other's arms without unclasping
hands, turning back to back and face to face.
Unclasp hands, but continue turning in the
same formation. Gradually work away and
see if movement can be executed without the
partner as a guide, directing the turns merely
by the "feel" or sensation of movement.

c. With scarf.

Hold the scarf in the fingers of both hands,
taking near the corners so as to have a wide
hold. Turn the body under the scarf with the
same arm movements as were used, or as were
suggested when the body was turned with the
head against the wall. At first work for large,
free arm and back movements. Gradually
refine them. Drop scarfs and continue moving
in the same manner as when using them.

The value of working with a scarf and partner
is that it gives an opportunity for experiencing or sensing the spiral without a too careful
and perplexing analysis of its evolutions, and
without an active coördination of the parts.

d. With different leads.

Take with shoulder, arm, head, leg, and body
leads.

Exercises with the Body Moving as a Unit—Cont.

e. Combine c and d with appropriate foot work, that is, steps that can be well adapted to this movement of the body. Also combine with varying shoulder and arm combinations.

When doing the spiral turning with very small steps, it is an excellent practice to work with the feet tied together. This develops sense of balance.

Before taking the spiral with the "slide, step, leap" turn, step out the action slowly at first. (The teacher should be certain that the students have good back control, and satisfactory general coördination before they attempt the faster and more vigorous leaping turns.)

While studying the spiral turns it is a good time to distinguish between the turns of the body that result from its rotating on its long axis (spiral) and those that come from its spinning around with parts held tense. Try spinning:

(1). With arms out at side, shoulder high, and body in a twisted position for starting. Start spinning by taking a large swing.

(2). With one arm.

Let the weight come up on the toes and move the feet in very small steps just enough to maintain balance.

The effect of the direction of the force of movement on the arms, if they are not held too rigid, is that they are flexed and drawn in toward the body.

Exercises with the Body Moving as a Unit—Cont.

(3). With both arms starting the turn.

(4). With the body turning simply by its being carried around.

The force and speed of the turn depends on how vigorous and fast the steps
are taken. Stand on the toes and spin
around with little fast steps, gradually
work into running and turning, and leaping and turning. Try different steps,
and take in different directions. Vary
the arm positions.

In preparing lesson plans from the outline it may be
helpful to reveiw briefly the main factors that affect difficulty of control.

A. Body stationary.

a. Balance.

Exercises may be taken with or without
assistance for balance.

Support may be derived from partner, or
from working in circles having every other
one assist, or from a chair or the wall.

b. Size of base.

Feet placed forward or sideward.

c. Height above the base at which movement
is being executed.

d. Complexity of movement.

Proceed from simple to complex.

e. Change in accent, speed and energy, and
amount of effort in antagonistic contraction
of opposing muscles.

Exercises with the Body Moving as a Unit—Cont.

B. Body in Locomotion.

Here the problem is the transference of weight from one foot to the other. The legs are not only supporting the body, but carrying it through space. The aim is "a carrying over" of the coördinated body movements. Not only must the body move in a coördinated, plastic manner, but it must be sensitive to, and capable of responding to an ever changing base. A constant adjustment to balance is a necessity.

Movement in locomotion is made more difficult by—

a. Decreasing the amount of body surface touching the floor.

b. Increasing or decreasing the height of the upper part of the body above the moving base, and changing the position of the upper body with relation to the lower (leaning far to the front, or to the back, or to the side).

c. Changing speed of transference of weight.

d. Changing the pattern or steps of the moving base.

Take through the primary steps, walking, running, leaping, hopping, galloping, skipping and sliding; then combine these into larger units— such as the polka, schottische, waltz, and original patterns. Further difficulty and novelty may be added by change in direction and leads.

For an example of progression from localized control with the body stationary to complete coördination of the whole body in locomotion the control of the body moving with the shoulder lead will be developed. It will be observed that this is only one example of the limitless variety of combinations that are possible, once the working principles are understood. The possible combinations of steps, leaps, hops, runs, skips, gallops, slides, bends, turns, and pauses with which any mood may be finally expressed are infinite. Since this particular problem is the "shoulder lead," to avoid too much repetition, let it be understood that the movement always is to start in the shoulder, and that the progression will be from one arm to the other, first alternating in opposition, then both together.

A. Body stationary.
   a. Spine fixed.
      (1). Lying on the floor, face down, with arms at side resting on floor.
         (a). Raise arms through lateral plane to full extension overhead. Pull arms down to starting position. Palms out. Palms facing.
         (b). Same, lifting the arms off the floor and carrying them through space.
         (c). Same (with arms at shoulder level), lifting arms off the floor as high as possible. Pull them down to starting position. Palms down.
      (2). Lying on one side.
         Take all movements possible in all directions and planes.
      (3). Sitting up.
         Head forward on one knee to keep the spine fixed.

(a). Hold arm at different angles to the body; in front, overhead, at side, in back. Take rotation combined with flexion and extension. Arm moves on its own axis. Refine the movement as much as possible without stiffening the arm. Aim for a complete "follow through."

(b). Same, carrying the arm through space, raising it forward, upward, backward and downward, and reversing.

(c). Same starting with arm at the side, shoulder high, carrying it across in front of the body and reversing.

(d). Make combinations of varying heights, moving in the different planes.

b. Spine Free.

(1). Side leaning rest. This partially frees the spine.

Repeat the shoulder and arm work directing the movement so as to have rotation, flexion and extension, and lateral bending of the spine, all within the limits of the position.

(2). Sitting up.

The head is free and the spine is now free except at the pelvic end. Circumduction may be added. Since the shoulder and arm work continues to be the same, only the positions will be suggested.

       (a). Tailor fashion.

       (b). Back on heels.

       (c). Feet at one side.

    (3). Kneeling.

       (a). On both knees.

       (b). Half kneeling.

    (4). Standing.

       Broad base.   Change size and position.

B. Body in locomotion.

  a. On floor.

    (1). First Roll.

    (2). Second Roll.

    (3). Third Roll.

    (4). Crawl.

  b. Standing.

There now enters the problem of moving in space in the different directions, a problem however which adds variety and the possibility of new meaning. It is necessary to distinguish between "the legs carrying the body" and "the legs following the body." One problem is to have the whole body follow the shoulder lead, which initiates the movement, and "pulls" the body after it.

Direct movement in the following paths.

    (1). Straight line—going forward, backward, sideward, turning. Vary the moving base by changing the step and tempo. Walk, run, leap, hop, skip, gallop, slide. Make sequences of steps as in the waltz, schottische, and polka. Invent new "patterns."

(2). Circle.
   Same.
(3). Spiral.
   Same.
(4). Curved lines, a continued "S".
   Same.
(5). Zig-zag line.
   Same.

All these movements may be varied by change in intensity and speed of execution. Every opportunity should be used to carry all control from merely mechanical to expressive movement. In all the exercises aim at measured movement with different "punctuation." Watch also the quality and orderliness of effort. Combine in series, turning with accent alternating from one shoulder to the other, then changing the direction by moving straight forward, making a "two-part rhythm" to one phase, or developing a three or a four part by adding new directions and combinations, or by repeating and rearranging repetitions of the two-part series. This may be done to waltz time, *Moszkowski's* "Waltz in E," for example. The development of such a problem is most interesting and leads to many personal discoveries.

The student who has done all of this preliminary work thoroughly has a satisfactory mastery of his body, and a complete range of movement at his command. He is now able to control the source of a movement and relax opposing muscles so that the movement may "follow through," that is, may, when initiated in any one part of the body, continue to the climax without obstruction, or inhibition. The result is a harmony of rhythmical coördinations that will carry far beyond the dancing class into all the various activities of life.

So much for the bodily training and preparation, the outward appearances of this dancing. The physical being must of necessity be perfected but primarily to serve as a well ordered instrument correctly tuned and sensitive to the impressions of the mind. Though there results from such a process, or should, great freedom and abandonment of movement it is entirely erroneous to think that this type of dancing is a combination of erratic movements and gestures distributed at random. It is this type of movement which the study and practice of fundamentals seeks to eliminate. The freedom sought and gained is the result of perfect control, not the result of unguided abandon. The controlled individual is the free individual—one who knows how to work because he is sure of his medium.

But he has gained more than this mastery of movement, more probably than he is aware of. For the unstrained balance and soundness of the nervous system that results from such rhythmical coördination of the body is of far more value to the individual in meeting the complex and often disturbing demands of life than any mere strength or skill. Then, too, during the acquisition of such a state of general physical well-being, the dancer has come to some understanding of the power and wonder of the physical self, and has learned to use that newly discovered self with respect and consideration.

He has also made gains of a subtler, more purely mental type which are not so easy to estimate. In his absorption in the movements of the body he has mastered he has gone far along the road to overcoming that most restrict-

ing of all handicaps, self-consciousness. He has also
found a new resource, the delight of free and expressive
movement with a body that responds joyously to the
slightest impulse of thought and feeling. And, finally,
in such perfection of bodily response he has found a new
source of beauty, with endless promise of still richer
experience to follow.

Chapter V

THE CONTRIBUTION OF MUSIC TO THE DANCE

 It is quite possible to dance without music, and there are some enthusiasts for the dance who are ambitious to restore it to its rightful place as an independent art. But there is such a special and organic relationship between the two arts, and so much to be gained from building on that relationship, that the teacher of the dance will want to open its resources to her students. For music came from the dance in the beginning, from the rhythmic impulse of man, and took from the dance the basic elements of its form and structure. But since that time music has made such advances that it has left the dance far behind. Therefore today we may go to music to experience the full realization of the possibilities of the dance.

Like all things, music has grown by minute increments. It has taken centuries for the first cry of joy or pain, and the first beating of sticks, which marked the rhythm of the early tribal dance, to become fused and elaborated into the melody, the harmony, and, only recently, the symphony. And it has taken all the resources of man's science and culture to develop the crude rhythms of the first music into the glorious symphonies of the last century. That is one of the reasons why the student of the dance will find the almost endless variety of musical

147

pieces, from the very simple to the very complicated, so helpful.

Probably of all the arts music makes the most universal appeal to man's interest. Its rhythms and its harmonies satisfy one of the most fundamental needs of every normal human being, the need for satisfaction of the sense of rhythm that is grounded deep in his physical constitution. But music does more than that. True, it works through its mastery of sound and rhythm, but that is not the secret of its power. Of all the arts music makes the most direct appeal to the emotions. In fact, it is in essence a presentation of emotional experience fashioned and controlled by an overruling intellectual power. So it comes to our ears today, freighted with all the emotions of mankind. Because of its wonderful suggestive powers, none but the best music should be used. Much might be written on the psychology of music, but time and space permits it to be only touched upon here. Those who teach dancing should read much and carefully the helpful literature available.

By suggestion music speaks to our feelings, and brings forth the unknown things that we have long felt, and gives voice to our gaiety and our sadness, our grief and our joy. It is this power of music as an emotional stimulus that makes it the most important of all the partners of the dance. The dancer by responding to the stimulus of the music can translate its sounds back into the emotions which inspired them.

But while the immediate impression of a piece of music is emotional rather than intellectual, and while the dancer, like any performer, passes the musical composition through the medium of his own personality, yet, if he is to make

Photo by Geo. Bell, Milwaukee, Wis.

Courtesy of Woodley Studio, Madison, Wis.

the most of it, he must be able to understand as well as to appreciate what he hears. For this reason, the student of dancing must have some grasp of the technical fundamentals of music.

It will, of course, be impossible for the teacher to give to each student a complete understanding of music, but she will be able to help him to acquire a thorough knowledge of tempo, accent, rhythm, melody, and to learn something of the history of its development into harmony and symphony. She will begin by trying to give him the values of the note, of the beat, then of the rhythm and change of emphasis, and finally of the grouping of sound into measures and phrases. When this much of the structure of music has been understood and the need of a well-developed sense of form realized, the student may commence to unite the fundamental steps (walking, etc.) and the note values of the music into groups according to the phrasing of the piece. At this time no attention need be paid to the content of the music, for what the students are working for is to develop their sense of form and their ability to respond accurately to the music. Every student must be able to find his own rhythm in the exercises before it is safe for the teacher to set a rhythm for the whole class, or for the students to try to dance together. Later the meaning of the various sounds may be studied and thought about, and the student may try to express in movement the message of the music, and recreate the composer's theme in his dance.

The ultimate aim of the teacher, therefore, is merely to help the student to appreciate the structure of the music, and to keep his dance in form and content harmonious with that of the music which stimulates and regulates it.

The deeper the student goes into the technique of music the better able will he be to hear and express each variation of pitch and intensity. And the more he studies its history and composition, the more will he appreciate its richness and meaning, and the more of its spirit will he carry into his dance.

The following is a suggested plan of procedure from the simple to the more complex steps of mastering the fundamentals of music. In it, as in the other outlines and suggestions given, room has been left for the initiative and originality of the teacher. The aim at first is to give only a general understanding of the simple structure of music, and through movement to develop a consciousness of its fundamental characteristics.

I. Give simple and clear explanation of the structure of music.

Demonstrate with block notes or by using the blackboard.

II. Listen to a piece of music having a pleasing melody and a marked accent.

A. Notice that:

1. The melody rises and falls.
2. Some notes are loud and others are soft.
3. Some are given more time value than others.
4. The loudest notes recur regularly, marking off measures, and giving metrical accent.
5. There is a further periodical recurrence of an accent marking off larger groups of sounds. It is like the pause in poetry marking off lines and half lines. The object is to separate groups of sounds containing a more or less complete musical idea and so constituting part of a

rhythmical phrase. This is the rhythmical accent, which appeals especially to the intellect.

6. Lastly, there are accented notes which occur apart from the metrical or rhythmical accent in what Lussy describes as an "exceptional and unexpected manner, disturbing the regularity and monotony of the meter or rhythm." These are the expressive accents, which appeal chiefly to the feelings, emotions, and sentiments. They give color, life, and expression to the music.

B. Let the students scan the music. Chalk and blackboard may be used, or the students may trace the movement and mark the accent with hand or foot on the floor.

III. Melody.

Give short talk on tonal relations.

Distinguish between following and responding to pitch.

IV. Tempo.

(The rate or degree of movement in time.)

For our purposes it will only be necessary to consider tempo under the three principal headings, slow, moderate, and quick, each, of course, in varying degrees. The power of rate of movement to arouse emotional states has been explained as a phenomenon of attention and anticipation. In slow time there is a voluntary effort to sustain attention in waiting for the next accent. This demand upon the subject's effort is what gives to slow tempo its effect of heaviness. The agreeable sense of the moderate tempo is due to the fact that it falls in the range of certain physical rhythms, such as walking and the beating of the heart. In the quick or rapid tempos, attention is involuntarily sustained, for the ear receives a quick series of sounds before they are anticipated. It is the supreme rapidity of stimulation that produces the lively and exhilarating effect of quick tempo. With the extremely fast tempos, there is a sense of the effort of trying to keep up.

A. Slow.

Gives feeling of heaviness, dignity, solemnity, breadth, gravity, and fullness. In compositions of this tempo the emotional element usually predominates. They are full of expression and sentiment. They also are good to give the student a feeling for melody.

Examples—"Largo," *Händel*; "Funeral March," *Chopin*; "Prelude," *Chopin*, Op. 28, No. 20.

B. Moderate.

Easy, graceful, moving, controlled, flowing. Gives sense of ease and poise without the heaviness of slow time or the haste of rapid time. Walking, running, and most dance rhythms, fall in this tempo. Such compositions are usually rich in melody and rhythm, not too complicated, and irregular, yet full of variety and contrast. Waltzes, Polkas, and Schottisches, in fact most of the music useful for our purpose, is written in this tempo.

C. Quick.

Vivacious, stimulating. May be stirring or most delicate and dainty in its suggestions. Requires brilliant and careful execution. The emphasis is more on the rhythmical and metrical accent than on expression. Such music is good to stimulate the student to rapid and accurate foot work.

Examples:—"Visions," *Schumann.*
"Tarantella," *Heller.*
"March" from "Concert Stück," *Weber.*
"Invitation to the Dance," *Weber.*
"Cracovienne," *Paderewski.*

V. Time.

(The rhythmic combinations or divisions of the notes).

A. Consider relation of accent to beat and measure. The accent measures off the beats into bars or measures and gives time; that is if the accent occurs on the first of every two beats, we get 2–4 time; if it falls on the first of every three beats, we get 3–4 time, etc. (Explain difference between waltz and mazurka).

B. Make clear the distinction between beat and note. Explain with note blocks or with blackboard.

C. Note time values. Sitting still, take each note with hands or feet. (A note is here considered as a unit of musical construction).

1. Even note values, that is, the notes follow each other at equal intervals.

a. Whole notes—4 beats.
b. Half notes—2 beats.
c. Quarter notes—1 beat.
d. Eighth notes—½ beat.
e. Sixteenth notes—¼ beat.
f. Sounds so close that change of position on each note is impossible.

2. Uneven note values, that is, the notes follow each other at unequal intervals.

    a. "Dotted-eighth and sixteenth" notes—1 beat.

    b. " Sixteenth and dotted-eighth" notes—1 beat.

    Distinguish between the two.

        Music that illustrates the difference:

        "May Day Gallop" and "Wah-wah-taysee."

VI. Just as we have taken a note as the unit of music construction, so we can find an analogous unit of construction for dance steps in any one of the following instinctive, elemental activities; walking, running, leaping, hopping, skipping, galloping, and sliding. As a working definition we will consider any transference of the weight from one foot to the other, as in walking, running, leaping, and galloping, or from one foot to the same foot, as in hopping and skipping, or from both feet to both feet, as in hopping on both feet, an elemental activity.

A. Even locomotion. This corresponds to even note values; that is, the steps follow each other evenly.

    1. Walking.

        a. Slow, taken to whole notes—4 beats.

        b. Faster, taken to half notes—2 beats.

        c. Normal walking, taken to quarter notes—1 beat.

        d. Very fast walking, taken to eighth notes— 2 to 1 beat.

    2. Running, taken to eighth or sixteenth notes.

    3. Leaping, taken best to quarter notes. Explain.

4. Hopping, taken to quarter or eighth notes, also to "dotted eighth and sixteenth" notes.

B. Uneven locomotion. This corresponds to uneven note values; that is, the steps follow each other at irregular intervals.

1. Skipping, taken to "dotted eighth and sixteenth" notes. (Is hopping in uneven time.)

2. Sliding, taken to "dotted eighth and sixteenth" notes.

3. Galloping, taken to "dotted eighth and sixteenth" notes. (Is leaping in uneven time.) Note that body is raised off the ground in contrast to the slide.

Try the above to "sixteenth and dotted eighth" notes.

Each one of these elemental activities should be executed in every possible direction, with different leads. This is to give variety and contrast. Work individually. Work in groups of varying numbers. Have each group take a different elemental activity and try out as many different formations as possible. For example, let one group take skipping, another hopping, etc. Progression is made from one step to another according to a previously worked-out plan. Use music of different tempos.

VII. Give a discussion on the more familiar so-called "dance-forms": Waltz, Mazurka, Minuet, Polonaise, Polka, Schottische, Gavotte, and March. Combine different elementary activities developing the Polka ("* Rosamund"), Schottische, ("*Dance of the Sprites"), Waltz (*Schubert*), Mazurka ("La Czarine"). (For explanation of starred selections see Bibliography of Music.)

VIII. Suggestions for developing the feeling for *Metrical Accentuation* through movement. Use different time. For 4/4 time use "Shepherds All and Maidens Fair." Work in groups of four, one student for each beat.

A. Have each student respond to his beat with some gesture or movement, giving the beat its exact time and value.

B. Substitute the different elemental steps on the beat.

C. Respond by fast turning, checking movement exactly on the expiration of the beat.

D. Combine action and pauses.

E. Proportion different note values to the beats.

F. "Rolling Hoops," stroking on the different beats.

G. Dramatize action according to the number of beats in a measure.

H. Catch and throw the beat from one to the other. Add interest by using different parts of the body. (Much originality is possible here). Class may work in large or small groups.

I. Number class according to the number of note values to be used, each number taking a different note value. Use some good 4/4 time, e. g. *Hollaender's* "March in D Flat." Change in mathematical progression.

J. Work in groups and have each student take a different step. Vary the number of the group and the steps according to the number of beats in a measure.

K. Make a "pattern" combining note values and pauses. Work out with dramatic content.

L. Have the pianist play one kind of note value and the class execute a different kind. For example, the pianist plays a lively skip, and the class runs. At call, they exchange. The pianist plays a "run" and the class skips. (Many combinations are possible here).

M. Snap fingers as though using castanets. Vary the force of the snap on the different beats. Music: "Fantasy Piece," Opus 26, *Schumann.*

N. Clap hands as in the use of tambourines, Music: "With Castanets," *Reinecke.*

O. Balance and contrast steps, using different time; for example, take 4/4 time.

　1. Have class substitute skipping for the first four beats, then run the next four.

　2. Tell them to skip for the first measure, then run as long as they have skipped. (The object is to discover if the class has realized that these are identical).

　3. Build sequences of movement to phrases.

P. Cultivate local response of body to music.

　1. Lying on the back.

　　a. With feet in the air have the feet respond to the music. "Sensitize" the feet.

　　b. Rest the elbows on the floor with the hands free; have the hands follow the music. "Sensitize" the hands.

       c. Have the whole arm follow the music. "Sensitize" the arm.

    2. Sitting up. Respond with head and upper body.

    3. Stand and dance with the whole body responding.

IX. Rhythm.

(The perfect, complete, and adequate expression of the human sense of equality, proportion, balance, symmetry.) Suggestions for developing the feeling for *Rhythmical Accentuation*, which gives structure, form and design. Attention is drawn to the structure of phrases and to the periodical recurrence of groups of bars which form symmetrical designs.

A. Contrast *time* and *rhythm*.

(Bad phrasing is like bad punctuation and bad accentuation in reading or speaking.) Note the systematic grouping; the repetition; the pause.

B. Discuss the need of form in any art.

Apply some of the suggestions given in VIII, using the half phrase and the whole phrase as points of division instead of the measures.

    1. First have class sit down and listen, attending only to the phrasing. When they have found the division, ask for some simple response at the beginning of each new phrase—such as taking a deep breath or clapping the hands or saying "Phrase."

    2. Work for half phrase, distinguishing between the importance of the punctuation at the half phrase and at the whole phrase.

    3. Take some objective point, such as a stool or a

wall and have class dance away for a half or whole phrase, then back at the end of phrase or second phrase. Work for accuracy and precision; it must be accomplished in the time allowed.

In this, space, time, and action must be judged.

4. Vary the above by

a. Gradually increasing the distance, while keeping the amount of music constant. In their effort to cover the ground the students spontaneously indulge in large and energetic action.

b. Gradually increase the amount of music, keeping the distance constant. The result is an impromptu adaptation by moving in spirals and circles, retracing steps, and taking many combinations of directions to "use up time."

Such problems are very interesting to the students, because they bring in an element of fun and also give them confidence in their ability to meet the sudden exigencies of the dance. Further interest may be added by using scarfs or balloons— dancing with them for a phrase or half-phrase, then dropping them at end of phrase.

The purpose of such problems is to adapt action to the limits of time and space. Many other suggestions might be given, but the above are sufficient to make the principle clear.

5. Change step (polka, skipping, running, waltz-

ing, sliding, etc., on the whole phrase, half phrase, and on the measure.

6. Form groups of 3, 4, or 5. Have one student the leader for a phrase, or for any length agreed upon; let the others follow him and respond to him; then change leaders, etc. Music: *Chopin*, "Prelude"—Opus 28— No. 7; "Valse Lente" from "Coppelia."

X. Development of style and taste in execution—"the faculty of giving to expression the amount of force, fire and life, proportionate to the intensity of the impression"—*Lussy*. Vary character of movement.

A. Crescendo.

B. Diminuendo.

C. Staccato.

D. Flowing.

E. Gentle.

F. Strong.

XI. Study a short selection of music, such as "*Schubert-Study," for its fundamental characteristics. Do not lose sight of the content in studying the form.

A. Musical accentuation—instinctive appeal.

B. Rhythmical accentuation—intellectual appeal.

C. Emotional appeal.

D. "Pattern."

The aim of this exercise is appreciation. Appreciation implies intelligence. If this important element is lacking, the experience is that of enjoyment and not appreciation.

XII. Take a two or three part instrumental record, ("To a wild Rose," *MacDowell*, harp, violin, cello), and have the students follow each instrument individually, and then work in groups of three, with one student in each group following his own instrument. Aim for accurate response and for harmonious movement. In this way a very lovely group dance can be created.

When each student has once learned to follow his own instrument in the harmony, there are almost no limits to the ability of a class to build a group dance rich in expressive beauty. Such skill, however, is attained only after long hours of practice.

XIII. Try several selections of music to dance "at sight." This means improvisation and spontaneous activity. "A la Bien Aimée," "Salto Mortale," "Schön Rosmarin," "Caprice Viennois," *Chopin*, "Waltzes," *Chopin*, "Preludes," "Elfin Dance," "Ecossaisen." For other compositions refer to bibliography of music.

From such a study of the fundamental principles of music, there should result a more thorough understanding of its structure and a deeper appreciation of its meaning and beauty.

Chapter VI

DANCE COMPOSITION

When the teacher approaches the problem of teaching her class the construction of the dance, the first and most important thing for her to remember is that what she is teaching is not a certain number of set dances, but a creative art. In the old schools of dancing the instructor had the children memorize the dances as the arithmetic master had them memorize their multiplication tables. Under such a system dancing became a mere routine of imitation.[1] It gave the dancer plenty of chance to display his skill in the reproduction of steps which somebody else had devised, but

[1] The disparagement implied in this sentence does not of course, extend to all forms of imitation. There can be no question of the value of imitation which understands the meaning of the action of another and sincerely enters into his motives and appropriates that action as the expression of a similar mental state. It is really learning by observation and suggestion. Thus understood imitation is one of the most important of human responses. For it is by means of this tendency to imitate the acts of those about us that the child becomes adjusted to his physical and social world. In this way imitation becomes the cement that binds people together with common ideals, sentiments, and standards. But we must also bear in mind, that along with this innate tendency to conformity there exists the tendency to individuality and the former must not be developed at the expense of the latter. Therefore, it is the leader's task to see that what is set up for imitation is worthy of being imitated, and the followers' to realize the true significance of imitation that he may more wisely select that which he wishes to emulate.

of opportunity for real creative work, it afforded almost none. It is in this respect that the dancing which we are teaching differs most radically from the conventional forms, as its appeal is neither to memory nor imitation (in the narrow sense), but to the creative instinct. What we are working for is not just skill in execution, but artistic expression of the individual dancer's own personality. It is the imagination of the dancer, therefore, that assumes primary importance in our plan for this stage of the work. All too often the word imagination is used in a loose and general sense for sheer fabrication without any searching regard to the mental processes that give birth to it. When thoughtfully used, imagination means no mere play of the mind beyond the confines of reality, but an important factor in the development of all mental life and in the development of all art. For it is imagination that pushes out beyond the narrow limits of our actual experience, by shaping and re-fashioning and extending the old elements of our past experience until we have an insight and an understanding that far transcends what we have actually seen and known. But although new combinations result, there are no new elements. The material of all imaginative activity whether it concern sense impression or inner mental state (especially feeling which plays so great a part in understanding and sympathy) is supplied by our past experience. Obviously, then, one of the limits of imagination is set by experience. But only one. For not all the experience in the world will enable the prosaicly unimaginative to envisage a step beyond his own narrow yard. Something more than mere experience is necessary. What is needed is that mental activity which builds upon experience. This the teacher of educational dancing must always remember. All the subject matter that we give to the student should be considered as to its power of stimulation, and we should challenge our suggestions as to whether or not they will call forth a creative response. After all, to be accurate we cannot teach anything; the meaning of education is to "draw out." What we can do and what we try to do in teaching dancing is to arouse an interest and an enthusiasm that will inspire the student and make him want to learn, that will result in his making the needed effort to discover within himself the hidden treasures of his own experience. The teacher cannot experience life for her student, but there are certain resources upon which she can call to interpret to him his own experience and to deepen and enrich his response to life.

So much of the success of this work depends upon the individual's expressing his own reactions directly that the question of whether it is better for him to work in a group or by himself must be considered. There are undoubtedly times when group work is of greater advantage, because when a student is working with other people, the rhythm of the group helps to free him from self-consciousness. On the other hand, when the element of emotion enters in, and the expression of personal feeling becomes the main consideration, the individual is apt to be hampered by a group or even by a partner. For the sake of freedom of response, then, it is best for the individual to work alone when he first undertakes self-expression in the dance. Then when he has acquired experience in working out his own reactions to a piece of music, for example, he may try to increase his powers of adaptive response by working first with a partner and then with a group of three. In time the students will discover among themselves harmonious rhythms, and building on these will create their own group dances. In this way each student will learn the fine art of subordinating his personal peculiarities to the larger purposes of the group effort without losing his own individuality.

In the beginning of their work the students will usually enjoy sheer rhythmical movement as they experience it in skipping, galloping, the polka, or the schottische. They will find it interesting to invent new steps by combining these elemental steps into larger units. Soon, when they have learned to emphasize structure and design, they will have simple group dances of much charm. These elementary dances may be made still more delightful both to watch and to do by the use of scarfs and balloons. Their use has already been suggested for making the fundamentals more interesting and more difficult. The student may, for instance, begin his work with a balloon, by using it to develop body extension. He may work for elevation of the chest by using the chest to keep the balloon in the air, or he may throw it up and hit it with his knee. He may also achieve full extension by tossing the balloon high and lifting his whole body in the effort to touch it while it is still beyond his reach. If he desires more complicated movements he may place it on the back of his hand, letting it roll softly down his arm, across his back down to the tips of the fingers of his other hand. Even such a seemingly simple movement requires subtle control of the back if the movement is to be at all times graceful and flowing. With these major movements and the appropriate minor ones he may create a simple dance.

Other interesting problems can be worked out on the kneeling base or on any of the various bases. The action of the balloon may be varied by resting it on the back of the hand and rolling it up and down the arm according to the direction of the movement of the body, or resting it on the palm of the hand. Or the student may wish to experiment with holding the balloon in various positions while he dances, as well as tossing it and letting it bounce. By dancing across the room in groups of three or four the students may easily give to each other suggestions for carrying and holding the balloons. Two students may dance with one balloon or with two balloons; three or more may work with one or more balloons, each group finding its own reaction to the music. Countless other formations may be made, with the balloon still inviting them on to invention.

Likewise, with the scarf it is possible to work out an endless variety of movements, some vigorous, others gentle. When used with vigorous music, the scarfs may be held in numerous ways, which the teacher will suggest from time to time. For instance, the end may be held in one hand and the entire scarf thrown over the shoulder with vigorous movements, which originating in the muscles of the shoulder and back follow through to the scarf, resulting in a whirling circle of color. With the advanced students two scarfs may be used. All this is, of course, not dancing; it is merely gaining the control necessary to dance. There are, however, countless lovely dances which the students may build out of these preliminary exercises with one scarf, two scarfs, one or more scarfs and a group of students, a large scarf and many students, and so on. If they are permitted to do so, the students often enjoy working with the balloons or scarfs before or after class, especially if it is possible for them to have a musical accompaniment.

In this way the beginner's desire to "do a dance" as soon as possible may be satisfied in group dances that do not involve too complicated steps, but do afford an interesting variety of design. Especially are such dances satisfactory if they provide rapid, vigorous movements, for these are the most accessible to beginners.

The more usual way, however, for a beginner to approach the construction of a dance is through an appreciative response to a piece of music. For our purposes, the piece chosen may be of two sorts, what may be called program music or what may be called absolute music. The first is more or less dramatic, inspired and inspiring by the aid of extraneous suggestions. The second simply embodies the rhythm of pure harmony. In either case, the music must be studied for its own sake, for one cannot truly appreciate any piece of music unless he experiences again to some degree the emotion which the composer is trying to express. But while the dance embodying the rhythms of pure movement is in the end harder to do successfully than the more dramatic dance, it is better in working with beginners to take up first the problem of simple rhythmic response without any dramatic complications. Then the more elaborate problems may be approached with the knowledge and surety gained from success with the simpler.

"Fanfare" is a good piece to take for one of the first class problems in working out a piece of music. It may be worked out more informally than most compositions. Since it is a short piece, it does not demand such sustained or such concentrated effort as a longer piece would. It is also rapid and stimulating in its movement with well marked phrasing and abundance of contrast.

The first part is well suited to the skip, the slide, the gallop, and the polka. In working on such a problem, it is wise to have as few students as possible trying the various activities at once. Have the class gather at one end of the room and number off, for example, by fours, Then have all "number ones" dance across the floor, then the "number two's," and so on. This not only gives the students more room for action, but also enables the teacher to observe each student's work. Moreover, it gives the students a chance to watch each other's work without any unnecessary embarrassment.

Have the groups dance across in turns with

1. Polka
   Forward, backward, and turn. Then in a series as, polka twice, turn around, then polka twice, going forward.
2. Skip.
   In the different directions.
3. Gallop.
   Same.
4. Slide.
   Same.
5. Different series, formed from 1, 2, 3, and 4, such as polka twice and skip four times, or four slides and four skips, or four gallops and four skips, all for the sake of experiencing different combinations.
6. After the students have studied the various combinations, let them dance the first part with what-

ever action presents itself spontaneously. Warn
them against monotony.

7. Repeat any of the above to test the accuracy of
their sensory discriminations; that is, let them
regulate their movements by the intensity of the
impression they receive from the music.

The next two phrases are especially good for the study
of rapid movement with an easing off of energy, and also
for the study of pauses. Because of the rapidity of the
movement, the novice is apt to be careless about observing the regulating force of the music. The ends of the
phrases afford a good opportunity for following pitch
and taking steps according to the note values. It is
helpful for the class to sing these phrases as they work
to them, at first standing still so that the body and arms
are free to follow the voice. Good results may be obtained
in this way. Since it is hard for those who are dancing
to sing, have the rest of the class give them a vocal accompaniment. In order to avoid any protests of inability
to sing, it is better to call this "vocalizing the movement."
Work for contrast by whirling for the first half of the
phrase, and "stepping" the note values and following
the pitch, for the last half of the phrase.

Have the music repeated, four phrases in all. Call
attention to the unfinished feeling of the first ending, and
the finality of the second. They may be likened to the
question mark and the exclamation point in the punctuation of written composition. After each phrase has been
studied, have the groups dance the phrases in order, that
is, have the number one's dance across with the first
phrase, then the number two's with the second, and so on.
Then, as they come back, have the number two's start

across with the first phrase, the number three's with the second phrase, and so on until each group has danced all four phrases. Then let each group take all four phrases, and finally the whole class together.

Any piece of music may be worked up in this way. It helps the student to develop a sense and knowledge of form. Although this is a simple problem, it contains all the constructive principles of more elaborate compositions. After the class has mastered the details of the problem, they should be given an opportunity to select and arrange these various elements that they have studied, and from them work up the form which best embodies their reaction to the music. This is a dance.

Another example of the simple group dance that can be given at first is a circle skip which is executed to the music of "May Day Gallop." Like "Fanfare," this satisfies the beginner's desire to do a dance. It also gives the class the joy of group participation and the opportunity of learning the fundamentals of structure, and while the teacher has the final result already in mind, she enlists the coöperation of the students, and has them help to build the dance. In every case she makes sure that the class understands why any particular development has taken place.

Have the class join hands in circles, preferably of eight, ten, or twelve, facing in, and number off by two's. Ask the class what this formation suggests. Some will say to skip around, and some will say to skip toward the center. Try both, and let the class decide which is the better for the opening figure of the dance. Usually the decision is to skip around. The next question to decide is how long and in what direction to skip. If phrasing has been studied previously, some will suggest skipping around for a phrase. If phrasing has not yet been studied, this will be a good time to discuss it. Before the class begins skipping, have them listen to the music for its phrasing, clapping their hands, or inhaling the breath on the first half phrase, and exhaling it on the last half. Then ask them to respond at any point in the music that seems to them a completed sentence. It will be discovered that there is confusion between the half and the whole phrase. In this particular piece of music the half phrase is very marked. Explain the difference, and make it clear that the half phrase, since it is so evident, should be recognized.

When the phrasing is understood, have the class skip to the right for one phrase. (Instruct the pianist to play just the one phrase.) Then ask the class what to do next. Some will suggest going on in the same direction for another phrase; others will recommend going back to the left. Try both. The class will discover that skipping back for a phrase gives balance. Now ask the class if they have a satisfying sense of completion, or if they feel the need of repeating what has been done. Of course, some will want to repeat. So this should be done. They will soon realize that in this case repetition makes for monotony. (Explain that there are times when repetition and monotony have their value). The first figure then is to skip one phrase to the right and one phrase to the left. Suggest that the strong emphasis of the half phrase be used to regulate the positions of the body, that is, that the first half of the phrase be danced with the chest and head high, and the last with the body bent forward. Have the class try the low position on the first and the high on the last half phrase. Then let them choose.

The class will be quick to suggest that they next skip toward the center, and that it will take only one-half phrase to go in, and the other half to skip back. They will want to repeat this for balance. Have them try the figure with hands joined and with hands free, and make their choice.

Now have the one's and two's face each other, joining either left or right hands. This breaks the circle into smaller units. The position at once suggests that partners dance around each other. Let them try skipping both for a phrase and for a half phrase before changing hands. They will find that skipping for a half phrase brings the change too suddenly. So a whole phrase is needed. Then this should be repeated with the other hands joined.

The last figure is somewhat complicated, but if the phrasing is carefully worked out there will be no difficulty. Have all the number one's face in and skip toward the center for a half phrase, then join hands and finish the phrase by skipping around to the right. At the same time the number two's face out and without joining hands skip around to the right for the whole phrase. In this way the two circles move in opposite directions. In this skipping around the number two's should skip wide of the inner circle in order that there may be some distance between the two circles. On the other hand, the circles must not be too large, since at the end the partners should be near each other. Now the partners skip toward each other for a half phrase, join both hands and spin to the end of the phrase, finishing their figure by taking strong extension on the last note.

In all they have danced eight phrases. While this

dance is simple in its structure, it affords ample opportunity for freedom and grace of action. The problem may be varied by doing this dance in smaller groups of four and even of two. Although made up of the same formations, the dance will take on new aspects as the number of the group decreases. And as the students gain better individual control and expression, the dance will gain fresh charm in its greater joy and spontaneity.

The dramatic dance brings up more complicated problems which will require careful study and preparation. First of all, the teacher must decide what to dance. As has been suggested before, the ideal is for the student to find his own theme as well as his own interpretation. But in the beginning the teacher will have to suggest the themes, a problem in itself, requiring both tact and resourcefulness on the part of the person who tries to solve it. For the themes must be carefully adjusted to the age and experience of the dancers, for only on the basis of their own experience can they make interpretations of any value. Then the teacher must take into account the varying temperaments to be found in her classes so that the dreamer, the mystic, the practical person, and the born comedian may all find opportunity to express themselves.

For these reasons, the teacher will find especially useful those types of material which afford interest and scope to students of all ages and tastes. A great deal of the classical music can be arranged in a simpler form to match simpler themes so that children will enjoy working with it. The older and more advanced students, on the other hand, will usually prefer to work to these pieces in the original rather than in simplified form. For the subtle varieties of the theme, which are lost in transcription, furnish the needed intellectual stimulus for enriching their dance. Often these maturer students require harmony and symphony rather than melody and rhythm. Children, especially if they are not too sophisticated, take great pleasure in impersonating the characters of Mother Goose and the nursery rhymes from "Old King Cole" to "Raggedy Ann." Older students will enjoy these, too, if they are approached in the right way. Two general approaches have been found successful. The first is to pretend that they are children playing king or doll. This is the more difficult approach because it makes two demands on the imagination, calling, as it were, for a rôle within a rôle, and because there are many people who get no pleasure at all out of pretending they are children. For the average older student, however, and especially for the adolescent student, it is better to let it be more reminiscent in character, for there are few people who do not enjoy reliving as directly as possible the joys of childhood, and most nursery rhymes have very pleasant associations. The rôle of the jovial monarch will be but intensified when the older student brings to it memories of his early conception of the King and his own added experience. It should always be remembered, however, that while nursery rhymes and other child verses give the child actual training in imaginary impersonation, and hence strengthen the imagination and the dramatic instinct, they are a means of relaxation to the older student and, therefore, should not be used too frequently. For the older student their greatest value is probably their adaptability to humorous treatment.

In choosing material it is also necessary for the teacher to keep her finger on the pulse of the class. On one day they may have come from an examination or some other strenuous mental work tired and restless. The music with smooth and flowing rhythm that will call forth strong, slow, rhythmical movements of the entire body will soothe and refresh them that day, where on a gray day on which they are inclined to feel depressed, they will need music of a much more sparkling and invigorating type. Then, too, the teacher will watch carefully to see that the simple group dances which please so much for a while are not allowed to pall, but are made to give way to dances that afford the indispensable intellectual stimulus and satisfaction.

As students become more advanced, they will enjoy finding their own themes, and then hunting up the appropriate music, to make out of the two their own dance. If properly encouraged, they will discover in their other classes resources which may be used for the dance. In their literature classes they may find poetry with definite rhythms which will afford almost as much stimulation to movement as music. And, if such efforts are made cordially welcome in the dancing class, they even bring in music and poems of their own composing which will furnish material for the dance.

A simple and interesting approach to the working out of these more difficult dramatic pieces may be found in the construction by the class of a simple dance from a piece like "Bacchanale." This is a good example of a dance whose forms and actions are suggested and molded by ideas from the outside. The music was originally arranged from several selections in order to get a musical expression of the idea. Then the music inspired a student [2] who had danced to it to write the following poem which gives a second expression of the idea. This is now used in the classes to inspire the third expression, the dance. In this way students experience the same idea in three different ways.

BACCHANALE

Oh wild free spirit, Bacchanale,
I see you dance from out the wood
And pause when you behold the arbor, heavy laden.
You gaze in breathless ecstasy.
Desire is born—you snatch the purple clusters from the
    vine
And with your twinkling feet
Stamp them upon the ground
To lie in bruised heap whose
Crimson juice bewitches. Ah,
How deep a draught you take
Of this enchanted wine!
Your rosy mouth a deeper scarlet grows;
You loose your spirit to the wind
And whirl away—
In madcap senseless passion.
With streaming hair and clapping
Hands you prance
In the abandon of your dance,
Then sudden stumble; leaping
High, you fall, and lie as
Some crushed flower, sleeping.

Begin by reading the poem to the class. The dancer's problem is to take the idea and let it mold and direct his movements. Then have the music played, and ask

[2] Miss Frances Ellen Tucker.

the class to follow it with action. To do this they should study it a phrase at a time.

They will soon find that the first two lines of the poem follow the first four phrases of music. The action is strong, vigorous, and joyous. To express this, the class works up a two part rhythm of leaping and skipping, four leaps and four skips, to which they can give variety by changing the direction and the accent (the intensity and speed) of their movements.

The next four phrases correspond to the next two and a half lines of the poem. The problem now is to find the appropriate action for the discovery of the grapes, to express the realization that they are all around, and the consequent arousing of desire. When working with younger students, the teacher must not ask too much of their imaginations. Sometimes, the class will be obliged to drop the idea in order that they may just follow the music. And in any event the teacher must guard against pushing them too hard with both poem and music.

The third movement of the dance is suggested by the part line "you snatch the purple clusters from the vine." This is developed in two phrases with high leaping and snatching of clusters and laying them upon the ground. Here the action should be just suggested. Any effort to represent it too literally violates the spirit of the dance, and breaks into the rhythmic grace of the effect.

The next two phrases are devoted to stamping in rhythm. Then at the line, "How deep a draught," have the class get down and drink with the dance coming over them more and more until they rise and finish with a deep feeling of exuberant life. The accompanying step can be worked out slowly by walking, and at the same time crossing the feet and getting a free twist of the body (the spiral) with a little extra step on the rear foot to follow the time of the music. When the rhythm of the step is mastered gradually increase the speed to the desired tempo. Clapping the hands over the head will give the necessary contrast. The dance ends with the dancer gasping for breath, pausing and falling exhausted to the floor.

Students enjoy the vigor of this dance, and they experience the elementary principles of dramatic dance expression which are fundamental to the more ambitious dances.

In preparing for more involved dramatic dances they will find it helpful to devote some time to the expressive possibilities of the dance. Like every art the dance has its own limits and its own ways. Therefore in all their work the students must recognize the necessities imposed by their medium. Not all moods are dance moods. Most of the elementary feelings, joy and love and hate and sorrow in their more obvious forms can be easily represented. And their subtler variations can be presented often with surprising effectiveness by the really skilled dancer. But it is doubtful if even a skillful dancer could represent so complicated an emotion as patriotism or some of the higher reaches of religious enthusiasm. In general, the dancer will find it easier to dance symbols than essences, for the province of the dance is what the body can express.

It is well for the teacher to insist on this limitation because the average student is not aware of the expressive values of bodily movement and position. He has little conception of how emotions energize the muscles, even of how his own feelings are reflected by the subtler movements of his muscles. For this reason, it is wise before the class has gone far in its attempt to construct dramatic dances to have it study the expressive values of various parts of the body. The teacher may take some movement, and then ask the class to take it to see if they have developed enough kinesthetic sense to reproduce a movement by the sympathetic feeling of it, or muscle sense of it. Whether they are able or not to reproduce the movement, this will give them valuable experience in reading muscle movement.

The class themselves will find it good fun as well as valuable practice to see what varieties of expressive movement they can work out within a given type. For instance, a class may see what they can do with the following for foot work on different types of bases. First, they can creep along as if they were going down a narrow passage with fear driving them on. Then they can see what the effect is when they do the same thing with the body flat. Then they can take the same series of movements with expectancy and surprise as the emotional elements. Or they can take the same movements as if in depression, or as if they were in old age, or as if they were working ahead vigorously in splendid health. Again, they may secure still more variety by exaggerating or burlesquing these movements. In all these ways, the class will secure control of the expressive possibilities of their own bodies and appreciation for those of others.

The study and imitation of beautiful movements affords students excellent practice, but in some ways, the study of humorous and comic movements affords even finer training. For comic movements unless they are controlled by taste and delicacy of feeling easily become vulgar. It is a nice test of taste and skill with expression to see if one can burlesque with grace. It means that every comic element must be preserved if the dance is to be effective, and yet must be subtly transmuted into the spirit of the dance if it is to please. Probably nothing demonstrates more clearly the superiority of suggestion to liberal pantomime for the purposes of the dance. Indeed, the secret of the never-failing appeal of the dance-comedy is its power of suggesting things quite beyond its scope.

The Mother Goose pieces, both the originals and those imitations that carry on their spirit afford ample opportunity for this type of work. The whole class should enter into the fun and see what they can contribute to the making of the comedy. A good problem for the beginners is "Old King Cole." This dance gives opportunity for a considerable number of the class to take part, for there are not only the jolly old King, and the pipe bearer, the bowl bearer and the fiddlers three, but for the purposes of dramatic contrast a court of eight or ten delicate and graceful ladies. The court can enter first with a graceful minuet step, and forming an aisle, face each other and end in a bow. Then the King comes in quite as jovial and gay as nursery expectations could demand. The ladies all bow, again with superlative grace. Then the King calls for his pipe, with a large gesture and the entire court takes the position of calling for the pipe with appropriate variations of grace.

Then a little page brings in with gay steps a large pipe, presents it to the King, and takes up a conventional position at his feet. In the same way the bowl is summoned, and brought. Then he calls for the fiddlers three. These three worthies enter, fiddling at a furious rate. They play, and the court dances. Then Old King Cole makes a gesture to show that the court is over, and starts out. As he goes, he looks at all the ladies in a fashion that makes it plain that he likes the ladies, and walks out immensely pleased with himself and everybody else, and with quite a little dance of his own in one foot. The pipe and bowl bearers follow, then the court, and last of all the fiddlers three, still playing vigorously.

Another dance that illustrates even more vividly the possibilities of suggestion in the dance comedy is "Captain Bing." The dance begins with a spectacular entrance by the Pirate Chief himself in a gloriously piratical costume. This costume like most comedy costumes is built on top of the regular dancing costume. A sash around the waist, a large black felt hat with the skull and crossbones that pirate etiquette demands on the front of the turned-up brim, and deep oil cloth cuffs over the dancing sandals leave no possible doubt as to our hero's profession. He comes in with a strut that puts his eminence in his profession equally beyond question, and pulls at his mustaches (he has none, but the gesture is so convincing that no one will venture to dispute him.) He pulls his cutlass, cuts somebody up, and tosses him away contemptuously. Then he calls up his crew. There are four of them, equally ferocious in the same picturesque fashion, with bandannas around their heads, curtain rings hanging from their ears, and gorgeous sashes of blue, orange, and red. They come to attention with a vicious gesture of knives thrust between their teeth (a hand serving as the knife). He puts them through their paces, hoisting sails,

and so on. Then he lapses into a brown study, gazing into
space. The crew with dramatic movements suggest
mutiny, and with most elaborate stealthiness sneak
toward him. But he turns, and they immediately change
their demeanor into one of studied innocence gazing out
to sea. Then he puts them through their paces again,
and they go out, leaping with a gesture as if they were
pulling up their piratical breeches, and disappear in a
hornpipe.

Such a problem as this offers wide opportunity for the
entire class to exercise their ingenuity on the various
incidental difficulties that arise in its working out. The
form of the dance presented above both as to its costumes
and its movements is the result of many ingenious suggestions from various members of the class, each of which
had to be tried out and worked over before it could find
its final place.

Yet suggestiveness alone, however clever, cannot make
a dance a work of art. Something more is needed—that
element of shaping, of form which distinguishes all art
from other forms of human activity. The student is
already familiar through his training in the fundamentals
and his first experiments in the making of dances with the
principle that the movements of the dance, however
spirited and spontaneous, are in no sense of the word
erratic. What he is now beginning to learn is that the
dance, fluid as it is, has its own artistic shape and its own
artistic principles. As Havelock Ellis says, "the dance
is the rule of number and of measure and of order, of the
controlling influence of form, of the subordination of the
part to the whole. That is what a dance is."

The dance lacks the element of permanence of form

that can be touched up and reproduced in a copy. It remains only in the visual memory of the on-looker and the kinesthetic memory of the dancer. Yet, just as much as any other work of art, it is subject to the general laws of unity or wholeness, and of organic coherence. A dance that presents discordant and conflicting elements in its final impression is no more successful than a picture that is made up of colors that clash. And a dance with no elements of contrast is no more effective than a novel without any conflicts of character or circumstance. A dance must have accent just as any other work of art must have some distinguishing mark of interest. So as students advance in their construction of dances, they will pay more and more attention to problems of form. They will experiment with balance and shading and accent, and they will try more and more to give to the expression of their reactions to life the beauty of form. And in doing so, they will be in no way sacrificing their main purpose of expression, for artistic form is not something extraneous and adventitious, but the most expressive form of self-expression. The most beautiful way of saying a thing is the truest way of saying it. Only sincere and earnest expression can give birth to artistic form, but on the other hand, only artistic form can do full justice to sincere and earnest feeling. For the spasmodic and aimless movement fails to satisfy the emotional need that gives it birth, and the incomplete and inadequate series of movements fail quite as much for self-expression as for art. Finally, the soul's own craving for beauty dictates that the dancer avail himself of whatever opportunity his medium affords for the pleasures of symmetry and proportion. In other words, dancing that shall really

Photo by Geo. Bell, Milwaukee, Wis.   Courtesy of Woodley Studio, Madison, Wis.

satisfy the human being's desire for self-expression must have artistic form.

All this implies, of course, conscious thought and effort. It is here that the dance requires genuine intellectual activity. But in all art the effort is not the goal. The artist thinks and works hard, but the reward of his effort is that moment, rare enough even in the work of the greatest, when out of the long labor comes the sudden perfect expression of his thought and feeling without any consciousness of the how or the why. So in the dance. At its greatest, the beautiful form springs out of the beautiful thought or the beautiful feeling without conscious premeditation on the dancer's part. Then we have the absolute dance, embodying the rhythms of the dancer's own feeling without the intervention of symbol or plan. But such power is in itself the fruit only of past effort. The surest way for the student who wishes eventually to achieve it is the slow, careful, painstaking, but nevertheless joyous and self-expressive method suggested here.

Chapter VII

THEMES

To do fuller justice to the important subject of themes than was possible in the foregoing chapter, a collection of dances used for the Dance-Drama program printed on pp. 285–291 are here set forth. As the titles suggest, these dances have been drawn from many sources— myths, legends, nursery rhymes, music, etc. The interpretation of these ideas has been the creative work of the students themselves, an expression of their personalities, a broadening of their sympathies and understanding, a temporary entering into the universal world of art.

In setting these themes[1] on paper, it has been the purpose throughout to avoid the set and detailed form which can be copied. Such copying with its parrot-like repetition of movement and gesture defeats, it cannot be said too often, every higher purpose of the dance. It is for this reason that in most cases the idea alone is suggested in hopes that it will prove stimulating to the originating and creative spirit of the individual. Even in the few cases where more minute directions are offered, it is hoped that no one will attempt the dance until he has wrought out his own complete intellectual and emotional conception of the piece. In other words, the directions here given

[1] The written form of these themes is the work of Miss Bertha Ochsner.

are to be used simply as stage directions are used by an intelligent actor.

FRIEZE

Music . . . ."Adagietto". . . .*Bizet.*

"Waltz," . . . .*Brahms*, Opus 39, No. 4.

Dance . . . . .In motionless contemplation, the dancers, grouped after the pattern of a frieze, hold a rope of roses, which garlands them together in bright tranquillity. As the music begins each spirit, still in her place, responds to the beauty of sound, with gentle sustained movements,—a subtle invocation of the Dance. Presently a more compelling rhythm is born, the irresistible rhythm of the waltz. And now the dancers, by ones and twos, fling aside their flowery bondage, and move gaily at will, each capturing a phrase for herself before she runs off to join her play-fellows.

Comment . . . . .A group of five or seven produces the best pictorial balance. The central figure should be standing erect at the introduction, with those on either side, in postures of gradual descent, thus following in general the sweep of an arc.

This dance came directly from the class work. Its unbroken flow of highly controlled and sustained movement could be liberated only after a thorough mastery of fundamentals. Then this understanding was deftly transferred into a more swift and capricious form.

NOCTURNE

Music . . . . .Nocturne . . . .*Chopin*, Opus 9, No. 3.

Dance . . . . .Here a single spirit comes, tuned like a lute of the gods, giving itself in utter harmony to the inspired will of master sound.

Comment..........In this case, the "Nocturne" was given to a class group as a problem in pure lyric movement, and the best interpretation so made was used for the public performance.

Run Run Run

Music.........."Le Secret" arr...............*Gautier*.
Dance..........One girl holds four others by silver reins tied to their shoulders in a formation that suggests Apollo driving the horses of the Sun. The horses leap forward joyously to the music; the driver reins them in, and they spring back for a moment only to dart forward again. So they curvet and caper and spin; they leap and gallop and run, always with the lightest of joyous grace, ever weaving from their fresh response to each impulse of the music, a constantly unfolding pattern of movement that delights the eye and lifts the fancy.

Comment..........It is somewhat amazing to find that this interpretation with all its elaborate continuity of action and infectious spontaneity, was gradually inspired from the most deliberate and painstaking execution of "foot-work," using first the walk, and then its more complicated deviations.

Mazurka

Music......"The Spanish Coquette".....*Blumenschein*.
Dance......Another dancer comes alone, translating

into motion the cadence of a melody, the pulse of a
rhythm, which strangely enough, in all the vast scope of
life is never twice the same.

Comment..........As in the case of Chopin's "Nocturne," this presentation was chosen from a group working out a like problem.

IDYLLIO

Music.........."Idyllio".......................*Lack.*
Dance..........Here is an idyl, born of mid-summer
fragrance, at such a time when dreams are delicate, and
the spirit of laughter is rather tenuous than gay.

The following order of movement has been worked out
for this dance:

1. Seven girls enter in line formation with shoulder to
shoulder, and faces turned ahead. They carry a rope of
roses about thirty feet in length, each holding it easily in
front of her at arms length. Since the rope is grasped at
equal intervals, the effect is as if it were festooned along
the line. They advance to the center of the stage with a
smooth yet moving step worked out to the music.

2. The center girl pulls the rope first to one side, then
to the other, and the dancers respond in fanciful movement to the force and direction of her pull. She then
advances, and the others follow. Then she starts the
pull back and the others follow, forming a circle as they
do so.

3. In forming this circle the dancers poise the rope over
head and put it across their shoulders, so bringing one arm
to the shoulder and the other forward to support the rope.

In this formation the group dances around with a step worked out to fit the rhythm of the music and the formation already made.

4. As the phrasing of this formation is completed, the circle opens, and as the rope unfolds, the center girl and girl second from each end come forward and dance. The other four hold the rope with the end girls dancing under it and the other two swinging rhythmically with very little movement. The three who have been dancing in front return, and the other four leave the rope to dance first in a formation of four and then in twos. They return to their places.

5. Finally, all take the rope and dance forward. They turn to the right (or the left according to the direction of the exit), place the rope on their shoulders, and dance off, all facing in the direction of the exit.

Comment......... In this dance one is clearly conscious of an ensemble feeling, that subtle sense which grows more true and sympathetic the longer the members of a group work with one another. One feels that double delight of a unity in movement combined with individual expression, in the presentation of a lyrical mood.

ARACHNE

Music.......... "Valse Triste" arr.......... *Sibelius.*
Dance.......... Under the curse of jealous gods, Arachne, once gay and lovely as a linnet's call, is now doomed to live in the detestable likeness of a spider. Perhaps to brim the cup of her agony, she is allowed a single hour of freedom, in order to taste again the felicity of her former

being. Then she must again bend to the burden of her consummate misery.

When first the music sounds, Arachne's soul struggles in pain and bewilderment, gradually becoming untangled from its fetters of ugliness, to the realization of an alloted solace, transient and bitter-sweet. With all the abandon of the young Arachne now dances the delight of a re-captured happiness. She moves in beauty, and her spirit is winged with joy. But ever and again, comes a faint ominous refrain of Fate, an insidious cadence of futility. Beating it from her with some new desperate joy, she dances on, always nearer the close of her fleeting hour. At length there comes an end. Again Arachne sinks helplessly into the cruel web that Destiny has set apart for her to spin, even so long as time shall turn.

Comment..........With this dance, the expression of a dramatic idea appears for the first time in this series of dances. It was inspired by a reading of the old Arachne legend, from which the most significant and poetic incident was subsequently isolated for presentation, and then a careful search made for music to coöperate with the dramatic content in the mind.

The Volga

Music..........Russian Folk Song—"Song of The Volga" arr.

Dance..........Against the hungry tug of a relentless stream, patient and uncomplaining, the stalwart boatmen shoulder the heavy rope that guides their craft to its mooring at the sedgy rim of the great Volga. At length, one last mighty effort brings it safely past the quickening current that eddies in sly treachery, there where white birches bend. They rest a little then, until the dawning of another day. In the strong rhythmic pull of their wracking toil, lies the beauty of combat with a vast elemental power, that seeks to shatter the spirit of man. Scarcely thinking, he then fashions a melancholy song to guard inviolable the precinct of his dreams.

Comment..........Here is dramatic content, and a second example of strong ensemble feeling, but one expressing a mood directly antithetical to the mood projected in "Idyllio." Where the latter was illusive and ephemeral, this is stoic and enduring. It presents in technical aspect, a poetic application of the so vital "back-work," constantly emphasized in class work. Seven girls were used in this presentation, forming a straight line well to the back of the stage. The rope was an imaginary burden. It is often far more effective to suggest material properties than actually to produce them.

SERENATA

Music.........."Serenata"..............*Moszkowski*.
Dance..........A melody, shuttled in silver thread through glinting fabric, is born a second time of moving loveliness.

Comment.........."Serenata" may be grouped with "Nocturne" and "Mazurka" in its genre.

Bacchanale [2]

Music..........Arranged.

Dance..........A young Bacchante, racing to sun and wind, breaks through the tarnished glory of full autumn. She leaps for purple grapes, high-hung on crimson vines. Then crushing them beneath the joy-mad beating of her foot, she drinks deep of their essence, winning her senses into driven rapture, and falls exhausted in her ecstasy.

Comment..........In no manner is this dance made an expression of conventional Bacchanalian revels, steeped in drunkenness. One meets purely the irrepressible joy in life, the abandon of avid youth to the infinite enchantments of beauty, which quicken the senses and sharpen delight in all things. Here dramatic content, though vital, is secondary to the expression of a mood. One is conscious of utterly unbound, and apparently undisciplined movement, but this very freedom finds its source in the most exacting exercises for the development of control.

Tarentella

Music........"Bajaderentanz" arr..........*Rubenstein.*

Dance..........Knowing full well the terrible edict of her fate, a peasant girl, stung by the venom of a tarantula, summons her companions, imploring them to dance with her to drive the fearful poison from her veins, that she may live the promise of her youth. Arms interlaced, the three leap forward, backward, circling in and out, spinning and swirling in a desperate combat with the tighten-

[2] Refer to poem, page 177.

ing snare of death. Exhausted, first one companion, then the other falls, rising in pain to battle still for the luckless maiden, doomed to die. But all is vain. The poison seeps its way to her heart, and after one last consummate struggle, she falls back lifeless into the arms of her half fainting companions.

Comment..........Here the demand for a perfect and difficult control is made, for, while the upper body must give an illusion of extreme fatigue, the feet and legs are called upon for a strong flexible support.

RENDEZVOUS

Music.........."Rendezvous" arr.............*Aletter*.
Dance..........Beneath the white enchantment of a far-swung moon, a shepherd and his shepherdess, fashioned from smooth, singing marble, stand poised on either side of broad, bright stairs. It is the garden of Versailles, whose past imprisons infinite echoes of light loves, and of fairspoken chivalry.

Now comes the faithful gardener, constant in his vigil, smiling a twisted, dream-like smile of things remembered, as he looks at the white lovers, and wistfully touches the rose caught between the slender fingers of the shepherdess.

Filtering the years, mingled with moon-magic, the sedate measure of a court gavotte threads the night. The gardener tries a step or two, but his bent back and knotted knees will not allow him to go on, and, seating himself at the roots of a near-by tree, the old servitor falls into a dozy dream.

Almost at once the still, white lovers breathe and turn,

and soundlessly descend the marble stairs, bending with
delicate grace, precise, fastidious, to the exacting rhythm
of the quaint gavotte. They dance again the tender
caprice of affection. The shepherdess, melting at length
to her lover's plea, throws him her rose, just as the gardener
begins to stir.

In a pretty panic, she twinkles back to her pedestal,
but held in his new rapture, her lover reaches his place
too late to return the rose.

The gardener, brushing his eyes, returns. Apparently
nothing has changed, and then he sees that in some
strange manner, the shepherd has become possessed of the
shepherdess' rose. Here, indeed, is a mystery! Ah well,
the past and the present; logic and fancy; dreams and
reality;—why seek to understand where one leaves off
and where the next begins? So thinks the gardener then,
and goes his way.

Comment..........."Rendezvous" owes its initial inspiration to a song of the same title. It was necessary
however, to make a special arrangement of the music,
and a really dramatic adaptation of the lyric.

SCARFS

Music......Waltz—from Faust Ballet—arr.......*Gounod.*
Dance..........Arcs of gold dart upward from an ever
changing source, now lending their burnished light to a
quivering swirl from the sea, to the rush of a comet's veil,
to the curve of an eagle's wing. Come,—fill your eyes
with a never still and never broken brightness!

Comment..........A frieze of five girls, moving vigorously over a stationary base, each with a scarf, forms a rythmic background for a single dancer, who with two scarfs works freely over the down-stage space. This poem of pure unhampered motion, came from an experiment made in class, when each member was told to work with a scarf in order to see for herself how much more beautifully it moved when the motivating action was completely relaxed and allowed to follow through without interruption from source to culmination.

JOLLY PETER

Music.........."Jolly Peter" arr......*Werner-Kerstein.*
Dance.........If life is not a pleasant thing, why live? Indeed the very object of existence is to be dapper, to be gay, to eat well, to sing much, to be light of foot, and above all to avoid dull dotards, who grow serious betimes.

Comment..........The strong individual appeal of this infectious tune, conjured up before one dancer in particular a very definite, rollicking jocular kind of personality. In comparing the presentation structurally with that of "Nocturne," "Serenata" etc., one finds a certain similarity, but elaborated by the projection of a fictitious medium, that is Jolly Peter.

LITTLE MISS MUFFETT

Music..........Arranged
Dance..........It is some moments before the main drama really begins, because it seems that the tuffet is in a state of sulks, probably caused from general overwork,

and doesn't want to play. Finally Miss Muffett trundles the stubborn creature to its proper place, and the well-remembered plot is fully enacted. After the spider has successfully routed his prim, young victim, a sympathetic chuckle passes between him and the disgruntled tuffet. They are both very bored with the game, and trust that it will be some time before Miss Muffett again feels the pangs of hunger.

Comment...........With the original nursery-rhyme as a nucleus, this childish ditty gradually became a new interplay of personalities, thus serving up delight to the sophisticated as well as to the innocent.

RAGGEDY ANN AND ANDY

Music..........."Funeral March of a Marionette" arr.........................*Gounod.*

Dance..........They are perfectly devoted, these two, but they find it acutely difficult to keep track of one another, chiefly because most of their time is occupied with pursuing that illusive principle in life, called equilibrium.

Comment..........After one glance at those delectable dolls, which now exist in every nursery, it is easy to understand with what spontaneity this dance sprang into being. Here the experiment of using masks was first tried with marked success.

I AM THE CAT

Music.........."I am The Cat".......*Charles Demarest.*

Dance..........He is no banal beast. He is none other

than Mr. Kipling's cat, who walks by himself and to whom all places are alike. He has been seen to arrange his regal tail for the purpose of solemnizing nocturnal hours, long, long before there were such things as house tops. During a brief feverish interlude, he secretely indulges in the potencies of catnip. This, however, is not generally known, for he is always quick to regain his most excellent composure. Again supreme, self-satisfied, a perfect isolated entity, he stalks indifferently into the night.

Comment. . . . . Kipling's "*Just So Stories*" provided the literary source of this fantasy, the attendant music then being composed especially to suit the theme. The appeal in such a study does not lie in the desire to imitate the actual aspect of a cat, but rather to endow that animal with human vanities, thus saving the presentation from mere mimicry and placing it in the realm of humorous satire.

CAPTAIN BING WAS A PIRATE KING [3]

Music. . . . . .Father Goose Rhyme. . .*Alberta N. Hall*.
Dance. . . . . .Scarlet adventure on high billowing seas.
    "The days grow dull, for I've not slit a brother's throat within the last long moon!"
Thus desperately complains one Captain Bing, pacing the deck and pantomiming his fearful impatience. He now summons four of his outlaw crew, who swing into sight with a rollicking hitch. But directly the Captain's back is turned, mutiny grows rife, and Bing pivots about on his heel, only just in time for the nipping of a plot

[3] See page 182.

which threatened his neck. With thunderous oaths, (fortunately silent) he commands the ruffians to action with renewed vigor, not to mention the frequent contact of cutlass and boot, until they show real joy at being ordered below.

Comment..........In the costuming of this serio-comic bit, the girls wore their regular simple dancing costumes, adding a bright bandanna, bound rakishly about the head. This costume by suggestion, rather than by specification, proved both more humorous and artistic in effect than a detailed pictorial reproduction of pirate accessories.

Visions

Music.........."Visions"................*Schumann.*
Dance..........A way to the moon is far. Perhaps a thousand nights of balancing from star to star would lead me there. Alas, those little points of light, atwinkle beneath my skipping feet, are but reflections infinite, on the smooth brow of an earthly pool. No, I shall never reach the moon!

So laments a small wistful spirit, wandering far, engulfed in the great greedy night.

Comment..........Here the delicate music of Schumann suggested not alone movement, but inspired besides, the projection of a longing so illusive, so fine-spun, that only the lightest touch might give it life.

An Harlequinade

Music.........."Amaryllis" arr................*Ghys.*
Dance..........It is May in the Bois, at the fashionable

hour of five on the boulevard. First a Gendarme, unhurried though businesslike, saunters his way directly across down stage. Now a tiny frilled and feathered lady minces in from the left back, dressed according to the dernier cri, and carrying a slim directoire cane. As she reaches center stage, a sleek Beau Brummel, high top hat and all, enters at her left, while to the right, a less comely figure puts in an appearance. With his cap scooped down across one eye, he perpetuates the inimitable swagger of the Apache. Deciding to favor the first, the little Flirt now casually drops her handkerchief, whereat the Dude makes quick use of his encouragement, offering his arm at once. As they walk along, he begins to recite an epic of his virtues, punctuated by grand gestures. This presently bores the capricious creature at his side, but in his complete self-absorption, Beau Brummel fails to notice that she has deserted him quite, to enjoy the marked attentions of his rival. Meanwhile the Gendarme paces off his beat (well to the back) unseeing and unseen. Then comes a smart slap with the glove. The Dude has sounded his challenge. There is immediate promise of a duel. The Flirt implores her suitors to desist, but both are deaf with rage. She then rushes off in desperation calling the Gendarme to her aid. The result is swift and effective. Both culprits make a somewhat eager exit, and the Gendarme, after just a moment of ethical hesitation, allows his arm to be taken by the languishing young lady.

Comment..........It is most vital in handling such a theme, that each of the characters be deftly presented, with infinite subtlety and grace, to emphasize its gay impertinence, and to avoid any possible suggestion of latent vulgarity.

THE FANTASTIQUE

Music..........*Charles Demarest.*

Dance..........A. Introductory Music.

B. 1. Two pages, dressed in short tunics, with waist-length capes hung at the shoulder, enter from left and right front wings. They dance in perky formal patterns, and then, 2. uncover a large gilded mirror, framed in an elaborate renaissance design of tumbling cherubs, which stands upstage to the right. This task performed, they skip to their places, downstage at the extreme right and left, and stand at attention.

C. Now the Court comprised of six or eight attendants, enters by twos in a precise minuet measure. Their costumes are of gay silks, fashioned after the edict of that period, with tight bodices and bouffant over-skirts. They end their dance in a tableau grouped about the wide steps leading to the throne, which is placed slightly off center well upstage.

D. A new motif, repeated at intervals as the drama proceeds, sounds the entrance of the Infanta, who dances then her childish vanity, preening before the long mirror. Finally she ascends her throne, commanding the entertainment, provided for the celebration of her birthday, to begin.

E. The pages announce in pantomime the arrival of a famous juggler, and resume their places.

F. Leaping and eager he comes, doffing his feathered cap, and runs the gamut of his amazing tricks. But the Infanta is only very meagerly amused.

G. The pages now gesture the announcement of a
second delectation. Two gypsies from afar, famed in
mysterious arts, attend the pleasure of their little sov-
ereign.

H. 1. They enter in a very maelstrom of abandon,
bending and swirling with swift sinuous movements.
2. Now they cease for a moment and come almost stealth-
ily to the throne telling of a vague evil fate that lurks
within the palace walls.   3. They continue their wild
dance.   4. They return again and prophesy impending
tragedy, born of a long journey from a far deep woods,
where once was happiness.   5. Another interlude of dance.
6. Then they foretell the coming of a strange surprise, a
thing more fabulous than any tale yet penned on parch-
ment.   The court shows real anticipation but the Infanta
scarcely listens.   7. With one last whirlwind surge the
gypsies disappear.

I. Pages announce the surprise—the pièce de resistance—of the day's fête.

J. 1. At the sound of his particular motif, the Fantastique makes an entrance upstage left.   He is hunched
and twisted, almost out of semblance to any human thing.
A little wild creature disheveled and unkempt, trapped
in a distant forest, he is now bewildered, struck with a
vast awe, before the glittering aspect of the magnificent
hall in which he finds himself.   2. Then he beholds the
Infanta, a picture far surpassing in its loveliness the most
extravagant of his dreams.   A deep, passionate devotion
flowers in his heart.   3. Desirous above all things of giving
what he can to heighten her happiness, the Fantastique
weaves his worship into a wistful little dance that is
awkward and angular.   At 4, 5, and 6, the fine ladies of

the court laugh in thoughtless ridicule at the pathetic capers and curvets of the poor misshapen creature before them. But the Fantastique understands nothing of this sophisticated mockery. He sees only that his efforts have brought laughter to the lips of the Infanta, and thus encouraged, his antics grow evermore fervent and spirited. 7. Now the Infanta in a moment of caprice, tosses him the crimson rose she has been wearing at the neck of her silver bodice. He catches up the token eagerly.

K. A duenna enters from the left and announces that if it please her Highness and the Court, the birthday feast is now in readiness.

L. Proceeded by the Infanta the Court now makes an exit, still tittering in derision, and the sound of their light mocking laughter echoes long after their departure.

M. 1. Now the Fantastique, alone in the great sumptuous hall, dances the sheer joy of his new-found happiness, with all the abandon that a crooked little body will allow. 2. Tenderly then he tucks away the rose into his tattered blouse for safe keeping. 3. Continues his dance. 4. Suddenly for the first time he catches the reflection of a grotesque figure in the great shining mirror. A muffled cadence of laughter comes from the feasting court. 5. He too laughs at this curious distorted image confronting him so boldly. But nothing can interrupt his delight for long and he still dances on. 6. Again the mirror startles him. This time he looks more closely and a terrible apprehension creeps slowly over his senses. In the deep woods there were no hard bright things like this and yet there comes the memory of a similar reflection that was wont to mock him often at the rim of a still pool. He frowns and waggles his tously head. There is a like movement from the creature before him. He shakes his fist and his tormentor threatens him likewise. The fear grows greater. He beats it off with frantic supplication, and prepares to try the ultimate test. 7. Breathing a desperate little prayer, the Fantastique takes the rose from his blouse. He knows there is only one such rose in all the world, and if the hideous creature in the hard bright thing is possessed of a like blossom, there will be but one answer to his last hope. 8. Trembling piteously he holds up the crimson token tossed him by the Infanta, and the cruel truth becomes known to his tortured soul. He understands at last the laughter of all those who beheld his ugliness. 9. Sobbing he falls into a little heap of rusty tatter,—to die,—just as the music reëchoes that tender, haunting melody born in his heart at the first sight of the Infanta.

Chapter VIII

THE PROBLEM OF THE PUBLIC PERFORMANCE

 So far our discussion has been mainly concerned with dancing for the dancer's sake, with little thought of the social factors that inevitably enter into even the most individualistic of educational activities. But as the instructor has probably discovered by this time, it is impossible to go far with any activity, around which so many preconceived ideas and expectations have gathered as the dance, without having to face the demands and expectations of people outside. These take their most harassing form in the expectation of some public performance or recital in which the students may display their skill and grace to an admiring circle of friends and relatives. The average parents are so used to having their children display their skill in dancing at least once a year, that they find it difficult to understand a theory of dancing which does not include occasional recitals, pageants, or exhibitions, and which insists that the raison d'être of the dance should be the pleasure it gives to the individual himself. Then, too, principals of schools often urge the dancing teacher to put on "exhibitions" as a means of securing public support for the new method of dancing. Finally, in many places, school activities

come to be regarded as a source of public entertainment, and the teacher who believes that public entertainment is not the purpose of the school is often put to it to escape the various requests for performance. Sometimes, she is called upon to furnish a brief dance program for an entertainment whose main spirit is far from congenial to an endeavor whose purposes are artistic in the best sense. From all these sources, then, from the parents to the managers of the yearly vaudeville show, the teacher will receive pressure for public performance, often when meeting such demands would seriously interfere with important educational processes or hurry into unwise exhibition students whose immature powers would be seriously injured by such forcing. The situation is still further complicated by the fact that students who are used to displaying their accomplishments, are often eager for the opportunity which so alarms the teacher. The instructor must face then the issue of whether or not her students are to be exploited to satisfy the egotism of the parents and the desire for entertainment of the community.

However much or little she decides to yield to these demands, the wise teacher will remember that a great harm is done to both the child and society when the grace and charm of the pupil are exploited, displayed and admired so that the pride of the parent in his offspring and of the teacher in her pupils may be gratified. As Findlay has said: "I need not enlarge on the moral perversion to which such an attitude (believing that the arts of music and dancing are solely designed for social pleasure) leads; it threatens the child's development not only as an artist but as a social being; he is tempted to regard himself as the

center of a circle; to find excessive gratification in self-
display instead of seeking values in art and society which
will raise him above himself."

There will come a time, however, when in the course of
their work the students themselves will naturally and
spontaneously wish to share with others the joy which
they have found in the dance. The little class recitals, in
which the members of the class are, by turns, audience and
performer, offer a delightful opportunity for satisfying
this wish, for in them the students can give to each other
the message each has received from the music. They also
furnish the student valuable practice in dancing before
others without becoming self-conscious and losing the
true spirit of the dance. In every way, these small
audiences of his fellow students are the best possible for
the student, for they afford him a dispassionate attention,
friendly but critical. If the true spirit of dancing is felt
and appreciated by the members of the class, they will
be quick to know whether a student is using the dance as a
means of personal aggrandizement, of "showing off," or
whether he is using it as a sincere medium of expression.
And if he is doing the former, they will soon make their
disapproval of such exploitation felt. And on the other
hand, with the older student who is more apt to be self-
conscious than egotistical, these groups of his fellow
students will afford a good audience for the first attempts
of shy sincerity. If such a student is not forced or hurried,
he may soon come to feel his fellow students' desire to
share their pleasure with others.

After a time the class may want to invite a few friends
in to see the dances which they have been working over
with each other. It cannot be said too often, that in-

formal occasions like this when the visitor sees not a special program but the actual work of the class afford a much better opportunity for becoming acquainted with the real spirit and method of the work than any possible public performance. But such guest nights while they afford the student the satisfaction of sharing his pleasure do not entirely satisfy the dramatic instinct which is so closely involved in dancing. Then too, the number of relatives and friends who can be gathered in by such a method must remain relatively small. Finally, the students may desire to attempt some larger group enterprise than the limits of the class hour permit. From all these points of view the most popular way of meeting this desire of students and friends for an evening dedicated to the enjoyment of beauty in movement is to have a dance-drama of some form.

The dance-drama is a more elaborate working out of a dance idea than the limits of the usual dance permits. It is more like a play, only in the dance-drama the various characters express the action by movement instead of words. As the third part of the program reprinted on page 290 shows, the dance-drama develops a definite action with contrast and variety, and above all climax. But even in thus emphasizing the dramatic nature of the dance-drama, we must remember that its distinctive nature is not drama but dance, that while it makes use of pantomime, it finds its center not in the expression of action but in the expression of feeling. The dance-drama is as suggested here, only a part of a longer program. This does not mean, however, that the program is just a heterogeneous string of dances. It should be definitely and purposively composed and organized. Experience seems to prove that it is wise to divide such a program into three parts. The first part is composed of shorter group and solo dances in which the material is comparatively abstract and moderately heavy, each piece leading to the next, with the entire series finding anticlimactic expression in the last. The second part consists wholly of more concrete "petites études;" among them usually several comedies based on nursery rhymes or similar material; while the third part is devoted to the dance-drama itself.

Obviously, such a program can do credit to an educational undertaking only if it is conceived of and executed in an educational spirit. It should find its material in the daily class work of the year rather than in specially prepared programs. The desirable evolution of a dance drama is from the daily class to the informal class recital, to the guest night, to the final public performance. If the class works on its smaller group dances during the year carrying them from the experimental to the guest night stage, the drama will have been practically built by the end of the year. It is not usually advisable, however, for students to work on these dances with this final aim in view. Dancing should always be an end in itself, and the student should devote himself to the joy of his work without any ultimate consideration of whether or not it is ever worked into a public performance.

The choice of dances for this program must of course be limited by the experience and the personal resources of the students themselves. But even with students who are not so far advanced those limits are wide enough to make it necessary and profitable to consider the problem of the choice of pieces for public performance. It may be laid down as a principle that only the best of music and of themes should be chosen for the public performance. Nothing else can do justice to the dance, and nothing else is really courteous to the audience. The nature of the audience must be considered, of course, but as a general rule, certain types of dance will not fail to make an appeal to the average audience.

In the first place, the average audience is made up of average people, that is people with a fair amount of more or less untrained imagination, who have come for an evening of entertainment and enjoyment. They are in no mood to solve elaborate puzzles in symbolism. And in this they are right. For the dance that requires much mental effort for its comprehension usually gives far less pleasure than the simpler dance which leaves the minds of the audience free to enjoy its beauty. Too much intellectual complexity is likely to prove a foe to æsthetic effectiveness. In general then, all other things being equal, an audience may be counted upon to enjoy most of the simpler pieces; even so simple a piece as "Run, run, run," when performed by one student acting as driver and four others as horses, has been welcomed with far more enthusiasm by an audience than much more elaborate compositions.

But to be effective, even the simplest pieces must have significant content. Either they should be clever, demanding action which is varied and interesting, or they should have depth of feeling and beauty of movement. The movement may, of course, be strong and intense, or graceful and flowing, but it must be of such a nature that the audience is given something which they may respond to and enjoy. If there is any doubt as to whether or not a dance or study comes up to the standards set it is better to omit it from the program.

On the other hand, it should be remembered in making out a program that too great a demand should not be put upon the emotions of the audience. There should, of course be variety in the emotional content of the different pieces; for instance, a heavy piece should be followed by a fanciful or humorous one. It should always be kept in mind, however, that the actual time between pieces is very short, and that the changing of the emotional state of an individual is a comparatively slow process. Therefore, there should be some preparation for the heavier pieces.

Every effort should be made to make the evening a thing of beauty. Artistic lighting and beautiful costumes greatly enhance the effect of very simple dances. So does sensitive and sympathetic rendering of the music. The printed program itself may strike the keynote of the evening. Whenever possible it should be printed attractively on good paper, unspoiled by advertisements. This will cost more, but the artistic tone thus obtained is worth the additional expense. Necessary descriptions of more elaborate dances may be put on this program. It is also often desirable to print little verses which express the mood of the different dances, and to introduce the whole with a poetical expression of the desire of the group to share with the audience the joy they have found in the dance. Such a program may be an artistic and desirable souvenir in itself.[1]

When the instructor approaches the problem from the point of view of the performers, the first problem she faces is that of casting the various parts. Here she must

[1] For suggestions see reprinted program, pages 285–291.

be sure that the students whom she selects are sufficiently developed in the study of the dance and sufficiently mature (this is not entirely a matter of age) to stand the pressure of rehearsals and the excitement of appearing before an audience or behind the footlights. If the dancers are immature, they are apt either to suffer from self-consciousness, or to fall into the common error of believing that the chief purpose of the dance is to amuse and to exhibit, and that they themselves should ever be the center of attention. As has been said before, the teacher of children may be greatly handicapped by the attitude of the parents at this point. In that case she is doing a kindness to the student to refuse him a part and to explain to him, and to his parents in terms that he and they can understand, the danger of a student's taking part in any kind of public performance before he has obtained sufficient mastery of his medium of expression and has developed his appreciation and understanding of the true spirit of the dance to the point where they can stand the demands put upon them by such a test. When she casts the various parts in the dance-drama, the teacher should pay careful attention to the individuality and peculiar characteristics, both physical and mental of the students whom she selects in order that the dancer's appearance and personality may fit the part which he is taking. When students are working in class, they should be given the opportunity to dance their finest dreams no matter how inconsistent the part may be with their physical build, but when it is a matter of public performance this factor must be taken into consideration. For while we may hope for the time when everyone will have the insight to see not only the actions of the physical person, but also those lovelier motions of the essential being within, still the fact remains that the average untrained person is as yet able to discern only what may be seen on the outside. It is necessary, therefore, for the actual, that is the physically visible, dancing to be in harmonious accord with the music and the demands of the part. The mystic may act the clown in class but let him be the dreamer or the seer in any program which the group as a whole may wish to give. On the other hand, to ask a student to be King Midas simply because he has the right build when the piece is distasteful to him and he values it merely as a class problem, is equally unfair to him. All of these factors must be taken into consideration if the result is to be as sincere and beautiful as it can be, and if the student is to gain from the production the joy to which he has a right. In so far as possible, then, the parts should be given to the dancers in accordance with their natural ability to react to and create emotionally and dramatically the part in question. For the more intensely the dancer feels the part, the easier will it be for him to transmit the emotion to his audience.

When it comes to coaching the dance-drama, the instructor must decide between the two alternatives of excellent expression or self-expression as the aim of her work. Detailed coaching, by one who has the imagination to picture the action in its entirety and who is able to call forth from the individuals the appropriate and needed action will, quite often, result in a real unity and finish. It is the method to use when excellence of expression is desired and there are too few in the cast who can, in the amount of time at their command, create the individual part so that it will harmonize with the whole.

But while this method can be used successfully with more advanced students who are able to make the instructor's suggestions their own without any great sacrifice of individuality, such a method is in general not educational and not consistent. To tell a student who has been accustomed to using his body to express his own reactions to the music, to watch the director and do as she does, or to follow a certain preconceived pattern, is to ask him to change suddenly his whole habit of thought, to side-track all the habits he has built up. However willing he may be, such side-tracking is not easily accomplished, and is necessarily detrimental to the spirit of the dance. A student's movements may be more perfect under such circumstances, but he will not get the joy out of the part to which he has a right. And the final work will be an expression, not of the personalities of the students working in harmony together, but of the director's personality only. It may be a lovely thing, it probably will be, but it will not have served the purpose for which it was originally conceived.

On the other hand, if we strive for self-expression, we shall often have to be content with less. We shall have to adapt our themes to the ability of our students, and be satisfied with simpler interpretations than we might make ourselves. We expect the student to do his best at all times, and, if he has been well taught, he will always wish to do his best. The best of a young student is, however, necessarily immature and unfinished. And the younger the student, the more patient we shall have to be with imperfections.

The most effective coaching from the educational point of view is that in which the teacher helps rather than directs the students in the creations of their own dances. Once the theme of the dance has been chosen, she will as far as possible leave the interpretation to the student, giving him no more suggestions than are necessary. There will be plenty of opportunity for her to bring her wider experience and her critical powers to his service. But in making corrections and suggestions the instructor will want to change the student's conception of the part, rather than his actions. For she knows that if his conception is right, and he has adequate control of his body, the gestures will take care of themselves. At the same time, the teacher will need to watch that the student does not become so absorbed in the presentation of a character that he forgets that he is dancing. The dramatic instinct with many people is stronger than the instinct to dance. It is often necessary, therefore, for the teacher to remind the students that all action, even pantomime, should be executed on a dancing base. In other words, where pantomime delineates literally, the dancer suggests only so much as is compatible with his medium of line and rhythm. Even where he needs to use pantomime, he must supplement it with dance steps that the organic form of the dance may not be broken.

In all this, the instructor will try to see the problem from the student's point of view. She will remember that a movement which may look ridiculous when she makes it, may be lovely when made by the student, especially by the child, and vice versa. And she will watch that the student does not imitate her movements or anybody else's without experiencing the feeling that gives them meaning. Neither will she encourage the student to make a movement of his that he does not really want to make. For not only must there be emotion back of a movement if it is to have meaning, but there must also be a compelling need of expressing that emotion. A person may feel joy, but if he does not also feel deeply the need to express that joy, any joyous movements which he may make for some other reason will be meaningless and ineffective. There is little danger in the class work that the student will make movements that do not spring out of emotion, that are not expressive, even if poorly so. In a program, however, he may realize that his art needs more action and try to give it action, while he is still vague as to what the action is expressing. It is necessary, therefore, to give the student plenty of time to comprehend thoroughly the part he is dancing, that he may realize in full the response which the music calls for. Once he has gained this realization, the appropriate action will come easily. If the instructor spends the greater part of her time and energy in helping the students really to feel the beauty of the dance and to experience sincerely its emotional content, they will not tend to make movements merely for the sake of the movement, but will use those movements which express that which they are experiencing. The result will then be worthy of the name of art.

But the dancer is not the only person who finds a part in the dance program. A successful dance-drama requires many different kinds of talent. The costumes and lighting afford students interested in those branches ample opportunity to contribute of their best to the beauty of the dance. The music affords opportunity to another group. The verses on the program represent the efforts of still another group or individual. But in every case, the individual contribution is subordinated to the whole.

The costumes and the lighting represent the best of someone's skill with design, or someone's sense of color. But it is understood that they are subordinate to the main purpose of the evening, the dance. At the same time, it is recognized that every effort, however small or obscure, contributes an honorable share to the success of the whole. No finer example of this, the spirit which makes a successful dance-drama possible, is to be found, than the girl who stands all evening by an opening in the curtains in order that the entrances and exits of her fellow students who are better able to dance than she may be managed as effectively as possible. That is the biggest contribution of the dance-drama to the experience of its makers. Each person does his part who gives of his best in whatever line, and the honor of the final success belongs to no one individual but to the entire group. It is for this reason that no mention is made of individual dancers on the program, and that the names of the entire group are printed in alphabetical order at the bottom. It is their best tribute to the spirit of the dance that the whole group coöperates to give the community something of the joy and beauty they have found with no thought but how they may best do justice to their purpose.

Chapter IX

THE LARGER ASPECTS OF THE DANCE AS AN EDUCATIONAL ACTIVITY

 To discuss the subject of this chapter, the "Larger Aspects of the Dance as an Educational Activity" is really to sum up all that has been said before in the course of this discussion in what may be considered a formulation of the fundamental purposes of this type of dancing. Such a formulation is of value to the instructor and her class because it presents briefly the purposes which should inform all our work and the values which should reward our efforts if they have been made in the spirit of these purposes. They are at once the justification and the incentive of our work.

Such a formulation if it is to be intelligible must of necessity be more categorical than is wholly desirable. For any statement of the ends of an art should be an organic synthesis rather than an analysis. Yet the very exigencies of its statement demand a dividing and a marshalling that however systematic they may be, must of necessity let slip through their interstices the finer breath and spirit of the undertaking. It is with an ever-present consciousness of this inevitable difficulty that this final formulation of the larger values of the dance is undertaken.

The first thing to be noted is that all artistic values to

be educationally significant must extend beyond the practice.

First of all, as cannot be said too often, the dance affords a source of pleasure to every normal individual. It is only recently that education has come to recognize the importance of recreation in the development of the individual, the necessity of providing everybody with some wholesome means of relaxation and recreation. Anything that affords a fresh source of pleasure is a genuine addition to life. Every normal human being enjoys the exhilaration of rhythmical movement, whether he is working in a group or by himself, and the sense of power that comes from the exercise of all his faculties in harmonious self-expression. And the pleasure is the more significant from the point of view of education in that the true lover of the dance can create its beauty for himself alone in a small room with a Victrola as well as on a stage with all the resources of a dance-drama.

This pleasure is also recreative in the best sense of the word. Too often recreation has been classed with amusement by people who have little respect for the great value of wholesome and refreshing amusement. But recreation is something larger than amusement. At its best it is a genuine re-creation, a relaxation of nervous tension, a freshening of interest and energy, a restoration of depleted powers. That is what the dance may mean. As one student has put it, "I can go into my dancing class tired physically and perhaps mentally, and actually feel rested and relieved. I don't know how to explain it in more æsthetic form, but I have a cleaned-out feeling." In other words relaxation is no mere flopping or collapsing of the body. It is not an end in itself, but a means to a

larger end, the winning of that poise which prevents useless expenditure of energy.   In experiencing relaxation
the aim should be to learn to use just those muscles which
are essential to a particular effort or movement.   In so
doing we relieve that stiffening of parts which constitutes
such a serious and unnecessary drain upon our energy.
Relaxation when properly used is a conservation of
energy, because it promotes the rhythmical flow of energy
through a body which is not inhibited.

Then, too, the dance contributes to the pleasure of
life in that it helps the individual to express himself.
Again, it is only recently that the necessity of self-expression to the healthy mental life of the individual has
been realized.   The average person tends to be con-
strained and awkward, and in certain parts of America,
largely because of the Puritan tradition, exceedingly
reserved.   Often his feelings are so effectually repressed
that they become thin and barren, and atrophied for
want of exercise.   Or often, finding no expression that
refines or transmutes them, they remain powerful but
crude.   Again, the average person is both awkward and
embarrassed in the presence of any call to totality of
physical expression.   There are few to-day who have that
fine coördination of body, mind and feeling which permits
them to move and act with any grace or surety.   The
average person finds his body, if not an expensive liability,
at least an instrument over which he has limited control
and with which he can express still less.   Every teacher
faces the problem therefore in both its forms, the fear of
emotion and of emotional expression, and the imprison-
ment of the personality in a stiff, unresponsive body.

Unfortunate as such a condition is in itself, it would

not be so disastrous if men could live without some emotional life. But they cannot. The emotional life of the normal human being must at once find some outlet of expression and some answering satisfaction from his fellows. But too often it is pent up within a hard and unresponsive exterior that repels rather than encourages the much desired fellowship of feeling. Here is where the dance, freeing the body from needless inhibitions, and breaking down some of the unessential reserves, frees the real man for a wider and more satisfying life.

In a more specific sense, the dance affords a medium of expression for those people whom Holmes has described in one of his poems as the singers who die with their songs unsung. There are many of these people who have beautiful things to say, but who can find no words for them. It is hoped that the dance may afford some of them a medium of expression that will give them the joy of embodying in a beautiful form some of the beauty within.

There is still another way in which the ability of the dance to afford the individual opportunity for self-expression serves his larger interests. Only in the present day are psychologists coming to understand those deeper emotional tensions that arise when powerful emotions must be left stopped within the mind with no opportunity for expression. Such an emotional tension often works havoc, where the same emotion understood and recognized with its energies transferred into some other channel becomes a source of personal power. Now it would be absurd to think that simply dancing a less powerful emotion could relieve one of these dominating tensions, but any form of free and joyous self-expression

© Bernice Oehler

relieves tension, and opens the channels for more free and unimpeded expression of other emotions. Moreover, everyone has had some experience of those wider transmutations of feeling that artistic expression may work. Overwhelming grief has been known to find its greatest solace in comic creation. And the exquisite heightening of consciousness that sometimes results from pain may find its greatest relief in entering sympathetically into the delicate and the whimsical. Any medium of self-expression that gives the individual the chance to enter through the gate of his own experience into a more universal experience to make out of his little personal experience a thing of beauty and of universal significance should serve widely and permanently the health of the emotional life.

At the same time, the dance should help to make the self which the student is trying to express a finer self. That is, the real aim of this type of dancing is the development of personality. Of course, the dance cannot put into the student what is not already within the scope of his natural powers and interests, but it can help to develop the powers he has in the direction of greater fineness and effectiveness. The physical effectiveness to which the dance contributes is a resource for the development of a higher type of personality, for almost as many mental as physical elements go into its making. But of more importance from this point of view is the power of the dance to help the student to cultivate his sympathies, to refine his taste, and to strengthen his preference for the finer things in art and life. These, especially the last, are notable services, for half the battle of conduct is the preference of the higher to the lower.

Moreover, in the dance, the student learns that the

narrower, meaner, more selfish and lazy self is not good material out of which to make art. He soon finds that the finer the self which he expresses, the more beautiful will be his creation. In the same way, he finds that the mere idiosyncratic expression of his own peculiarities does not make so interesting a dance for other people to watch as a more universal expression of his theme in which the elements find a wider validity than his nature affords.

That is one of the greatest services of any form of art—its power of carrying the individual beyond himself into a greater world of imaginative experience and understanding. There are few better ways of experiencing an emotion than by working it out in bodily movements. Such a problem makes the student more observant of the people around him, of the rich play of feeling that goes on constantly under the superficial surface of everyday life. And in this imaginative experience, he has a chance to become more understanding, more tolerant, more sympathetically respectful of the inner life of other people since sympathy is the natural fruit of greater understanding.

He may also secure from his dancing valuable experience of the working out of emotion in the lives of men, a knowledge that later may serve him well. Of course, no imaginative preconception of an emotional experience can ever do the reality justice in its fullness and its insistence, but it can make the student more sensitive to the impress of experience, and more intelligent in his reception of it.

Finally, the dance not only satisfies and enriches the student's sense of beauty in one form but in the understanding it gives him of the fundamental elements in all experience of beauty, rhythm, variety within limit, proportion, balance or symmetry, and unity and harmony of the whole, it carries him beyond the limits of one art into the wider realm of all art and makes him a citizen of its world of beauty and meaning. This is one of its greatest services for it ministers to one of man's oldest and most persistent needs. The history of art is the story of man's love for the beautiful, his search for those harmonies of form and meaning which would satisfy his craving for ideal perfection. When one realizes the struggles which the race has made, the numbers of times that it has fallen back into chaos, one acknowledges the gigantic power of this instinct which has led men out of the jungle and kept them resolutely on the upward path. Man's love of beauty is much like the thing of beauty itself; one can analyze and explain its parts, but there is always left over that intangible essence which men call spirit.

But even more important for this wider orientation than the knowledge of beauty is the attitude toward beauty which the dance helps to cultivate. For, here as elsewhere, the accessibility to experience depends largely upon the attitude with which it is approached. It is almost as hard to define the æsthetic attitude as to define beauty. Probably the most effective way of getting at its secret is to see how it works. The most significant characteristic of the æsthetic attitude is a detached, impersonal relation to the object observed. It is a "psychic distance" whereby the observer is enabled to appreciate the object as an object, judging it solely by its own appropriate standards. The æsthetic attitude enables him to love its beauty for the sake of beauty alone, with no thought of "possession, fame or success." It is only when the love of pure color, form, or movement is stronger, either as a result of natural capacity or of training, than the instinct to possess or the desire to win, that the æsthetic attitude is possible, that beauty can be "its own excuse for being." Obviously then, the æsthetic attitude demands a very considerable evolution and civilization of the personal instincts.

It is apparent from this definition, that the æsthetic attitude goes beyond art in the narrower sense. Indeed, there are few experiences toward which one could not maintain an æsthetic attitude, for there are few experiences in life which do not possess elements of beauty. We are so apt to make the mistake of thinking that only the fine arts contain these elements that we need to make the effort to remember that they may be present in anything from "the building of a house to the planning of an attack in football." He who has the æsthetic attitude recognizes this fact and appreciates these elements wherever he finds them, applauding the better artist in every field, even at the cost of his own material interest. Such a point of view will keep him from making the mistake of thinking that a work of art is great simply because it is expensive or is advertised as a model of the latest school, or is an expression of his favorite subject. The æsthetic attitude, then, is not determined by the object with which one is dealing, but rather determines one's relation to the object. It is a purely impersonal appreciation in the abstract of the difficulty of the problem, and the effectiveness and beauty with which it has been solved.

This valuing of things for their own intrinsic merit is the foundation of all the higher levels of human life. It

frees the individual from the fetters of place and circumstance, and gives to him the essential possession of all
that he can appreciate. And on the other hand, it may free
him from himself, from self-seeking, from jealousy, from
prejudice, and releases his energies for coöperation with
all his like-minded fellows in the creation and appreciation
of beauty.

This attitude toward art and life is the greatest contribution of the dance to modern education.

frees the individual from the fetters of place and circumstance, and gives to him the essential possession of all that beauty appreciates. And on the other hand, it may free him from himself, from self-seeking, from jealousy, from prejudice and releases his energies for cooperation with all his like-minded fellows in the creation and appreciation of beauty.

This attitude toward art and life is the greatest contribution of the dance to modern education.

Drawings

PLATE I

Fig. 1 is the illustration of a comfortable and practical garment that may be worn under any of the costumes. It is made of silk or cotton jersey. It comes in a flesh color so it can be dyed to match the color of the outside costume. It is so made that it may be worn without the costume when working on fundamentals, which is of great help to the instructor as it is then possible for her to see the action of the various parts of the body, especially those of the back. It is more comfortable also for the student not to be hampered by a costume when working on the floor.

Fig. 2 shows the skirt part of Costume A, which is made of two widths of forty-inch material. The length of material is twice the measurement from under the arm to below the knee, plus an extra inch for the casing around the top. Sew the two edges together about two-thirds the way down and run an elastic through the casing and adjust shoulder straps. The finished length of the costume should be such that when kneeling it just touches the floor.

Fig. 3 represents the top or overdrape of Costume A. The amount of material necessary for the overdrape is about twelve inches more than the length of the material in the skirt. For example, if the measurement from under the arm to below the knee is thirty-six inches, the skirt will take seventy-two inches, and the drape will take twelve more or eighty-four inches, the whole costume requiring about four and one-half yards. Cut an oval neck (*N*), leave two inches for the shoulder, and make a nine or ten inch arm slit on each side (*A, A'*). First put on the skirt, then slip the head and arms through the openings of the overdrape and fasten the shoulders to the shoulder straps of the skirt with clasps. A ribbon, or metal cord, or metal belt may be used around the waist. This costume may be made of crêpe de chine, tricolette, or georgette. The width, however, needs to be forty inches. It is an effective combination to use crêpe de chine for the skirt and georgette of the same color for the overdrape.

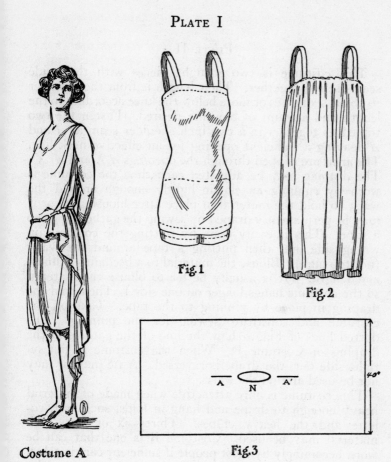

PLATE I

Fig. 1

Fig. 2

Fig. 3

Costume A

PLATE II

This costume is two straight pieces with their side seams sewed together. Their length is from the shoulder to about six inches or more below the knee according to the length and amount of blousing desired. Fasten the two top edges together in a two-inch shoulder seam at A and A' leaving a sufficient opening for an effective neck line. The arms are slipped through the openings $A X$ and $A' X'$. The draping may be adjusted each time the costume is worn by running an elastic lightly enough around the waist to hold the material in place after blousing it, or it may be permanently draped by sewing the gathering on to a tape. This is easily done by putting the costume on wrong side out, then putting a tape around the waist (not too high). Blouse the material to a becoming fullness and length. (It is usually better to blouse the material so the costume hangs longer on one side.) Then hold the draping in place by pinning to the tape. Take off the costume and substitute sewing for the pinning. The dotted lines of Fig. 4 show the line of the gathers of the draping of Costume B. When the costume is put on right side out, the drape is reversed. A tie may or may not be used around the waist.

This costume is only attractive when made of material heavy enough to drape and hang in folds, such as tricolette and the heavy crêpes. Thirty-six or forty-inch material may be used. Costume B is one that can be worn becomingly by most people if sufficient care is taken in the draping.

PLATE II

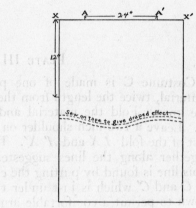

Fig. 4

Costume B

Plate III

Costume C is made of one piece of thirty-six inch material, twice the length from the shoulder to just below the knee. Fold the material and cut the neck opening N. Leave a two-inch shoulder on each side and split the rest of the fold $A X$ and $A' X'$. Tack the front and back together along the lines suggested by $C B$ and $C' B'$. This line is found by putting the costume on and pinning at C and C' which is just under the arm and far enough down to permit a comfortable armhole ($A C$ and $A' C'$). B and B' are holes cut through the front and back and through which the ribbon is drawn. These holes should be at the point which makes for the most becoming waist line. Crêpe de chine, tricolette, georgette, and silk and cotton crêpe are all satisfactory materials for this costume.

PLATE III

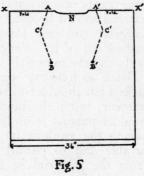

Fig. 5

Costume C

PLATE IV

This costume as illustrated is made of a piece of material thirty-six inches wide and two and three-quarters yards long. If a longer and fuller costume is desired use three yards of forty-inch material. Very soft and filmy material should be used for this costume, such as chiffon, georgette and raw Japanese silk that has the dressing washed out of it. Very effective costumes may be had by dyeing the materials in shaded colors.

Drape as follows:—pin the corner $L\ S$ at the top and back of left shoulder to the shoulder strap of a firm undergarment; bring the material around to the front of the shoulder passing it under the arm. Fasten $L'\ S'$ to $L\ S$ leaving the armhole large and loose enough to be comfortable and to permit an easy drape under the arm. Cross the material in front to the right shoulder and fasten leaving it loose enough to form the desired neck line. Carry the material under the right arm and up in back. Pin $R'\ S'$ to $R\ S$ forming the right armhole as before. Carry the material across the back to the left shoulder and fasten L^2S^2 to $L\ S$ and $L'\ S'$ so as to form a graceful neck line in back. The remainder of the material falls in a long drape from the left shoulder in back. The belt line may be adjusted either by tying a ribbon around the entire costume, confining the side drape, or the drape may be left hanging by running the ribbon through the material at "B." If a belt with a clasp is used no hole need be cut as the belt may be clasped through the material at the side.

PLATE IV

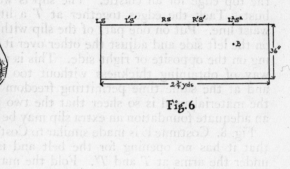

L^2S L^1S^1 RS R^1S^1 L^1S^2

•B

36"

2¾ yds

Fig. 6

Costume D

PLATE V

Fig. 7 shows one part of a two-piece slip which is the foundation of the long Costumes E, F. Take one width of forty-inch material of the desired length, which should be shorter than the outside costume. Run a casing along the top edge for an elastic. The slip is worn above the bust. Tack the edges together at T a little below the waist line. Put on one part of the slip with the open side on the left side and adjust the other over it with its opening on the opposite or right side. This is a very effective way of obtaining thickness without too much fullness, and at the same time permitting freedom of action. If the material used is so sheer that the two pieces are not an adequate foundation an extra slip may be used.

Fig. 8. Costume E is made similar to Costume C, except that it has no opening for the belt and is tacked only under the arms at T and T'. Fold the material as in C, cut out the neck N and slit the rest of the fold at A X and A' X' leaving a two-inch shoulder. After tacking, turn the Costume other side out—which brings the side draping inside. The material for this costume should be forty inches wide, very soft and sheer, such as chiffon crêpe or a soft georgette. The length should be so adjusted that the costume is becoming to the wearer.

PLATE V

Fig. 7

Costume E

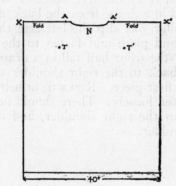

Fig. 8

Plate VI

Take two pieces of material forty inches wide and of the desired length. The size of the pieces used for the draping in the illustration is forty inches square. One inch from the top make a ten-inch slit down the center of each piece which forms the armhole A A'. At B a point about eighteen inches from the top of the material cut a belt hole. Drape as follows: Slip the right arm through the opening of one piece; take the point of the front piece and cross it to the left shoulder and fasten; the other part falls in a drape from the back of the right shoulder. In a similar way slip the left arm through the armhole of the second piece and fasten to the corner of the first piece. Let the front half fall in a drape and cross the other half in back to the right shoulder and pin to the shoulder of the first piece. Run a tie or belt through the belt holes and fasten loosely. There should be one drape in back falling from the right shoulder, and one in front from the left shoulder.

Plate VI

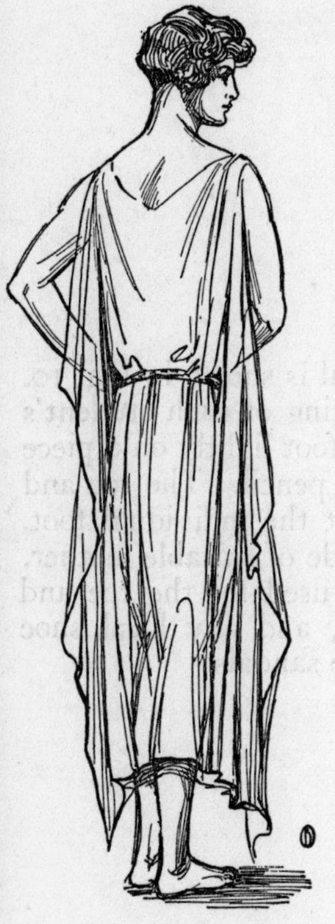

Costume F

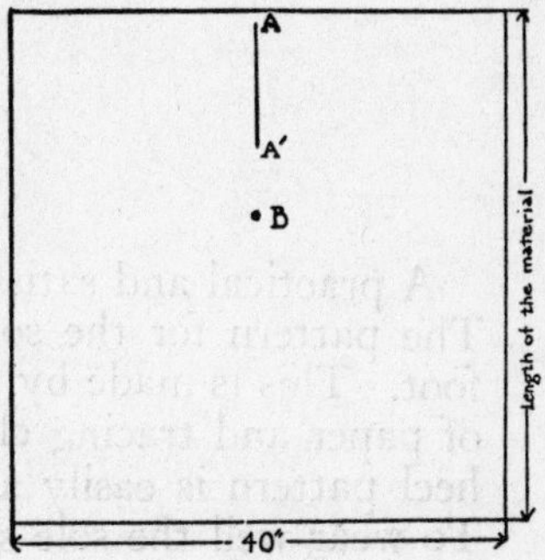
A
A′
B
length of the material
40″

Fig. 9

Plate VII

A practical and satisfactory sandal is shown in Fig. 10.
The pattern for the sole is the tracing of each student's
foot. This is made by pressing the foot lightly on a piece
of paper and tracing closely with a pencil. The toe and
heel pattern is easily adjusted to fit the individual foot.
To wear well the sole should be made of suitable leather.
A softer, but firm leather may be used for the toe and
heel. The pattern is easily made, and any local shoe
repair shop will be able to make the sandals.

PLATE VII

Sandal

Sole: Shape of your own foot.

Toe: —

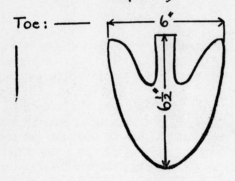

Heel: — Stitch together on dotted lines.

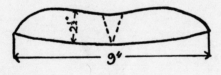

Fig. 10

Plate VII

Sandal

Sole: Shape of your own foot.

Toe:

Heel. — Stitch together on dotted lines.

Fig. 10

PLATE VIII. FIRST ROLL

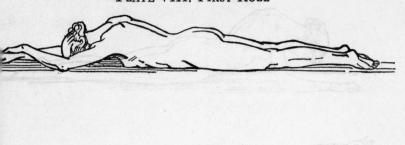

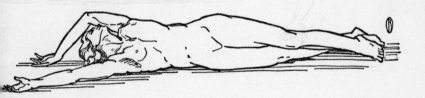

PLATE IX. SECOND ROLL

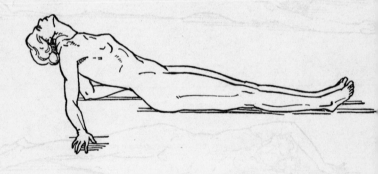

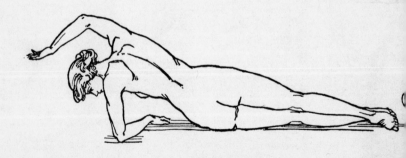

Plate X. Third Roll

(This last movement is taken in the opposite direction so as to show the action of the back.)

PLATE XI. UNFOLDING AND FOLDING

PLATE XII. UNFOLDING AND FOLDING (CONT.)

PLATE XIII. THE CRAWL (FORWARD)

PLATE XIV. THE CRAWL (BACKWARD)

(The last position of the backward crawl is the same as that of Fig. 1 with leg position reversed.)

Plate XIV. The Crawl (backward)

Bibliography for Reading

This bibliography is intended to be suggestive and helpful in a general way only. Divisions have been made in order that the material may be more easily found. No attempt has been made to follow this classification in the magazine articles.

I. PHILOSOPHICAL BACKGROUND

Alexander, F. Matthias—*Man's Supreme Inheritance.* E. P. Dutton and Co., N. Y.

Allen, Grant—*Physical Aesthetics.* D. Appleton and Co., N. Y.

Baker, James H.—*Education and Life.* Longmans, Green and Co., N. Y.

Brown, Geo. H.—*Esthetics of Motion.* Turner Pub. Co., New Ulm, Minn.

Cannon, W. B.—*Bodily Changes in Pain, Hunger, Fear, and Rage.* D. Appleton and Co., N. Y.

Carman, Bliss—*The Making of Personality.* L. C. Page and Co., Boston, Mass.

Clodd, E.—*Story of Primitive Man.* D. Appleton and Co., N. Y.

Curry, S. S.—*The Province of Expression.* Expression Co., Boston, Mass.

Curtis, E. W.—*The Dramatic Instinct in Education.* Houghton, Mifflin Co., Boston, Mass.

Darwin, Charles—*Descent of Man.* John Murray, N. Y.

Darwin, Charles—*Expression of Emotions.* John Murray, N. Y.

Davis, Henry—*Art in Education and Life.* R. G. Adams and Co., Columbus, Ohio.

Dearborn, Geo. V. N.—*Influence of Joy.* Little, Brown and Co., Boston, Mass.

255

Dewey, John—*Democracy and Education.* MacMillan Co., N. Y.

Edman, Irwin—*Human Traits and Their Social Significance.* Houghton Mifflin Co., Boston, Mass.

Ellis, Havelock—*The Dance of Life.* Houghton Mifflin Co., Boston, Mass.

Emerson, Ralph Waldo—*Essay on Art.* Nelson and Sons, N. Y.

Fiske, John—*Destiny of Man.* Houghton, Mifflin Co., Boston Mass.

Fiske, John—*Meaning of Infancy.* Houghton Mifflin Co., Boston Mass.

Galloway, Geo.—*The Principles of Religious Development.* MacMillan Co., N. Y.

Gordon, Kate—*Esthetics.* Henry Holt and Co., N. Y.

Griggs, Edward Howard—*The Philosophy of Art.* G. W. Hubach, N. Y.

Grosse, Ernst—*The Beginnings of Art.* D. Appleton and Co., N. Y.

Hall, G. S.—*Education Problems*, Vol. I, ch-2. D. Appleton and Co., N. Y.

Henri, Robert—*The Art Spirit.* Lippincott Co., Philadelphia.

Hirn, Hrjo—*Origins of Art.* MacMillan Co., N. Y.

King, Irving—*Development of Religion.* MacMillan Co., N. Y.

Kirkpatrick, E. A.—*Fundamentals of Child Study.* MacMillan Co., N. Y.

Kroeber, A. L.—*Anthropology.* Harcourt, Brace and Co., N. Y.

Knight, William—*Philosophy of the Beautiful.* Scribner's Sons, N. Y.

Langfeld, H. S.—*The Aesthetic Attitude.* Harcourt, Brace and Co., N. Y.

Munsterberg, Hugo—*The Eternal Values.* Houghton, Mifflin Co., N. Y.

Munsterberg, Hugo—*Principles of Art Education.* Prang Educational Co., N. Y.

Munsterberg, Hugo—*Psychology and Life.* Houghton, Mifflin Co., N. Y.

Noyes, Carelton—*The Gate of Appreciation.* Houghton, Mifflin Co., N. Y.

Patrick, G. T.—*The Psychology of Relaxation.* Houghton, Mifflin Co., Boston.

Plato—*The Dialogues,* Vol. 1 and 2; B. Sowett. Scribner, Armstrong and Co., N. Y.

Pyle, W. H.—*The Psychology of Learning.* Warwick and York, Baltimore, Md.

Ribot, T.—*Psychology of the Emotions.* Scribner and Sons, N. Y.

Robinson, J. H.—*The Mind in the Making.* Harper and Bros., N. Y.

Russell, Bertrand—*Philosophical Essays.* Longmans, Green and Co., London.

Russell, Bertrand—*Why Men Fight.* Century, N. Y.

Shairp, J. C.—*Culture and Religion.* Hurd and Houghton, N. Y.

Spencer, Herbert—*Essays, Scientific Political and Speculative—Origin and Functions of Music.* Appleton and Co., N. Y.

Stainer, Sir J.—*Music in its Relation to the Intellect and the Emotions.* H. W. Gray Co., N. Y.

Swift, E. J.—*Mind in the Making.* Chas. Scribner's Sons, N. Y.

Tagore, R.—*Personality.* MacMillan Co., N. Y.

Tanner, Amy Eliz.—*The Child—His Thinking, Feeling and Doing.* Rand, McNally and Co.

Thorndike, Edward—*Educational Psychology—Briefer Course.* Teachers College, Columbia University, N. Y.

Tolstoi, L.—*What is Art?* H. Altemus Co., Philadelphia.

Tylor, Ed. B.—*Primitive Culture—Researches in the Development of Mythology, Philosophy, Religion, Art, and Custom.* H. Holt and Co., N. Y.

Van Loon, Hendrick W.—*The Story of Mankind.* Boni and Liveright, N. Y.

Woodworth, Robert S., *Psychology*. Henry Holt and Co.,
N. Y.

II. MUSIC AND MUSICAL APPRECIATION

Custer, Ella W.—*The Sources of the Power of Music*.
The Mosher Press, Portland, Maine.

Dalcroze, E. Jacques—*Rhythm, Music and Education*.
Putnam's Sons, N. Y.

Downes, Olin—*The Lure of Music*. Harper and Bros.,
N. Y.

Faulkner, Anne Shaw—*What We Hear in Music*. Victor
Talking Machine Co., Camden, N. J.

Gehring, A.—*The Basis of Musical Pleasure*. Putnam's
Sons, N. Y.

Glyn, Margaret—*Rhythmic Conception of Music*. Longmans, Green and Co., N. Y.

Groves' *Dictionary of Music and Musicians*. Theo.
Presser and Co., Philadelphia, Pa. Edited by J. A.
Fuller Maitland.

Gurney, Edmund—*Power of Sound*. Smith, Elder and
Co., London.

Lussy, H.—*Musical Expression*. H. W. Gray Co., N. Y.

MacDowell, Edward—*Critical and Historical Essays*.
Arthur P. Schmidt, N. Y.

Mason, D. G. and Surette, T. W.—*The Appreciation of
Music*. H. W. Gray Co., N. Y.

Mason, Daniel G.—*A Guide to Music*. The Baker and
Taylor Co., N. Y.

Mathews, W. S. B.—*The Great in Music*. John Church
Pub. Co., N. Y.

Parry, C. H. H.—*Evolution of the Art of Music*. D.
Appleton and Co., N. Y.

Perry, Edw. Baxter—*Stories of Standard Teaching Pieces*.
Theo. Presser, Philadelphia.

Perry, Edw. Baxter—*Descriptive Analyses of Piano Works*.
Theo. Presser, Philadelphia.

Spalding, Walter R.—*Music: An Art and A Language*.
Arthur P. Schmidt Co., 8 W. 40th St., N. Y.

Trail, Florence—*Meaning of Music*. Richard Badger, Boston.

Wallaschek, R.—*Primitive Music*. Longmans, Green and Co., London: N. Y.

III. Dancing and Dancers

Caffin, Caroline and Charles—*Dancing and Dancers of Today*. Dodd, Mead and Co., N. Y.

Colby, Gertrude K.—*Natural Rhythms and Dances*. A. S. Barnes and Co., N. Y.

Dalcroze, Jacques—*The Eurhythmics of Jacques Dalcroze*. Small, Mayward and Co., Boston.

Dance, The—*The Art of Music*—Vol. 10. (Boni & Liveright, N. Y.) National Society of Music, N. Y.

Emmanuel, Maurice—*The Antique Greek Dance*. J. J. Little and Ives Co., N. Y.

Flitch, J. E. Crawford—*Modern Dancing and Dancers*. J. B. Lippincott Co., Philadelphia.

Grove, Lily—*Dancing*. Longmans, Green and Co., London.

Gulick, Luther—*The Healthful Art of Dancing*. Doubleday, Page and Co., N. Y.

Johnson, A. E.—*Russian Ballet*. Constable and Co., London.

Kinneys, The—*The Dance*. Frederick A. Stokes and Co., N. Y.

Marsh, A. M. and L. P.—*The Dance in Education*. A. S. Barnes and Co., N. Y.

St. Johnson, Reginald—*History of Dancing*. Simpkim, Marshall, Hamilton Kent and Co., London.

Terry, Ellen—*The Russian Ballet*. The Bobbs Merrill Co., N. Y. and Indianapolis.

Urlin, Ethel—*Dancing—Ancient and Modern*. D. Appleton and Co., N. Y.

Vuillier, G.—*History of Dancing*. Appleton and Co., N. Y.

Whitworth, G.—*The Art of Nijinski*. Robt. McBride and Co., N. Y.

IV. Miscellaneous

Beegle and Crawford—*Community Drama and Pageantry.* Yale University Press, New Haven.

Box, Wm. Sherwood—*Mythology of all Races.* Marshall Jones Co., Boston.

Bulfinch, Thomas—*Mythology.* Thomas Crowell and Co., N. Y.

Farrar, F. A.—*Old Greek Nature Stories.* Thomas Crowell and Co., N. Y.

Gayley, Chas. Mills—*Classic Myths.* Ginn and Co., Boston, Mass.

Hope, Thomas—*Costume of the Ancients*—2 vols. Henry G. Bohn, York St., Convent Garden, London.

Kahn, Otto H.—*Art and the People.* The New York City Shakespeare Tercentenary Celebration Committee.

Lee, Joseph—*Play in Education.* MacMillan Co., N. Y.

Luckiesh, M.—*The Language of Color.* Dodd, Mead & Co., N. Y.

Thomson, Arthur—*Anatomy for Art Students.* Oxford University Press, New York, London.

Watts, Diana—*The Renaissance of the Greek Ideal.* G. Arnold Shaw Co.

Weinberg, Louis—*Color in Everyday Life.* Moffat, Yard and Co., N. Y.

Magazine Articles

Art and Education: L. H. Wild. *Education;* 83: 159.

Black Butterflies: S. Hartman. *Forum;* 51: 294–304. F., '14.

Dalcroze Idea, The: M. Naumburg. *Outlook;* 106: 127–31. J. '14.

Dance, The: W. T. Benda. *Scribners;* Dec. 1916.

Dance, An Expression of Mental Activity. *Cent.;* 88: 823–33. O., '14.

Dance of the People: Mary F. Roberts. *Craftsman;* 22: 195–9. My., '12.

Dance Problem, The: Mrs. Chas. H. Israels. *Conf. Char. and Corr;* 1912 p. 140.

Dancing: J. Corbin. *Hampton;* 27: 97–104. July '11.

Delights and Disappointments aroused by Diaghileff Dances. *Cur. Op.;* 60: 175–6.

Emotion of Joy, The: G. VanNess Dearborn. *Psych. Rev.;* Vol. 2 No. 5. Apr. 1899.

Faun, That has Startled Paris. *Cur. Lit.;* 53: 208–10, Aug., '12.

Field Sports Among The Wild Men of Northern Luzon. *Nat. Geog. Mag.;* 22: 215–67. March '11.

Folk Dances for Health: O. Inglis. *Harpers Weekly;* 55: 13. July 8, '11.

Greek Drama and The Dance: G. W. Cornish. *Fortn. Rev.;* 99: 290–301. F., '13.

Is Modern Dancing Indecent? O. Inglis. *Harpers Weekly;* 57: 11–2. May, 17, '18.

Mechanism of the Emotions: Angelo Moso. In *Clark Univ. Decennial Celebration;* 1899 pp. 396–407.

Natural History of Dancing: Louis Robinson. *Cur. Op.;* 56: 364–5. May, '14.

New Reflections on The Dancing Mania. *Cur. Op.;* 55: 262–4. Oct., '13.

On With The Dance: O'Sheel S. *Forum;* 45: 189–199. F., '11.

Philosophy of the Dance: H. Ellis. *Atlantic Mo.;* 113: 197–207. F., '14.

Plea for a Scientific Mode of Dancing: Sir Ray Lankester. *Cur. Op.;* 55.

Problem The Tango Has Inflicted on The Church. *Cur. Op.;* 56: 206–56.

Psychic Processes and Muscular Exercise: Angelo Mosso. In *Clark University Decennial Celebration;* 1889 pp. 383–395.

Relation of Dancing to a Commercial Age. *Craftsman;* 26: 241–3. May, '14.

Renaissance of Dancing: Felix Clay. *Liv. Age;* 281: 195–207. Apr. '14.

Renaissance of Dancing: F. Youn. *Liv. Age;* 270: 532–5.
Renaissance of the Dance. *Harp. Weekly;* 56:6. Dec., '12.
Renaissance of the Dance. *Forum;* 46: 322–8. Sept., '11.
Revolution in the Ballet: *Lit. Dig.;* 47: 284–5. Aug., '13.
Rhythm and Recreation: J. Lee. *Conf. of Char. and Corr.;*
    1912, 126–19.
Shakespeare of the Dance: F. Toye. *Fortn. Rev.;* 98:
    1143–52. Dec., '12.
Significance of the Present Dance Movement: Lucia
    Gale Barber: *New Eng. Mag.;* 41: 272. Nov., '09.
Some Musical Analogies in Modern Poetry: *Amy Lowell
    Musical Quarterly;* Vol. VI.—I. Jan. 1920.
Sources of Our Popular Song and Dance. *Lit. Dig.;* 47.
Spanish Dances: A. S. Riggs. *Century;* 83; 389–400,
    J., '12.
Theory of the Dance: Anna Pavlova. *Harper's Weekly;*
    58: 14–S., '13.

Bibliography of Music

Realizing the difficulty most teachers experience in finding music, the following list of proven material is offered.

The selections starred (*) are special arrangements and may be obtained from Mrs. Mary A. Trumpf, 138 Breeze Terrace, Madison, Wisconsin.

Material in quotation marks indicates that the dance is given the name of the music.

Vol. II. and VIII. refer to "Piano Pieces the Whole World Plays."

Many of the selections may be found in record form.

This material should be obtainable from any of the following:

Breitkopf and Hartel, Music Publishers, 22–24 West 38th St., Bear Building, New York City.

Clayton Summy, Music Publishers, Chicago.

Ditson, Oliver, Co., Music Publisher, New York.

Lyon and Healy, Music Publishers, Chicago.

Presser, Theo., Music Publishers, 1712 Chestnut St., Philadelphia.

Schirmer, G., Music Publishers, New York.

Adagietto—*Bizet*.
> Fundamentals.
> Frieze work.
> Lofty, calm tender.

Ah! Sad My Heart—*Tschaikowsky*.
> Fundamentals.

Air de Ballet—*Chaminade*.
> "Dance Characteristique."

Allegretto "March Heroiques" Opus 40 No. 3 *Schubert*.
> Good rhythmical study.

A la bien aimée—*Schutt*.
  Good waltz for group dance.
  Lovely melody, graceful rhythm.
Amaryllis—*Ghy*.
  "An Harlequinade."
Andante Cantabile—*Tschaikowsky*.
  Fundamentals.
Andante Celebre, Opus 14, No. 2—*Beethoven*.
  Good rhythmical study.
Andante "Surprise Symphony" (2d movement)—
  Haydn.
  Light, gay.
Andantino—*Thomas*.
At Dawn—"William Tell"—*Rossini*.
At the Brook—*Boisdeffre*.
  "Dance for three"—"Danse au clair de Lune."
  Ethereal, tender.
Ave Maria—*Schubert*.
  Fundamentals.
Bacchanale—"Samson and Delilah"—*Saint Saens*.
"Bacchanale, The"—arranged.
Badinage—*Herbert*.
  "The Gossips."
Bajaderentanz—"Feramors"—*Rubenstein*.
  "The Tarantella."
Barcarole—"Tales of Hoffman"—*Offenbach*.
  Vol. II.
* "Bee and the Rose"—arranged.
(Mendelssohn's "Spinning Song," Drigo's "Sere-
  nade.")
Berceuse—*Delbruck*.
Berceuse—"Jocelyn"—*Godard*.
Berceuse—Opus 22, No. 23—*Karganoff*.
* "Big Brown Bear, The"—Adapted from song by *Mana
  Zucca*.
Bridal Procession—*Grieg*.
  Bright and gay.

* "Butterfly, The"—*Bentley and Loomis* in "Play Songs."
　Nursery Rhyme.
Calm, The—"William Tell"—*Rossini.*
Canzonetta—*Hollaender.*
　Gentle swinging rhythm in 6/8 time.
Caprice Viennois—*Kreisler.*
Capricieuse—*Elgar.*
"Catch me if you can"—*Concone*—arranged.
　"Pas de Trois."
Cavatina—*Raff.*
Circus Ring—*Filege.*
　Study.
Country Gardens—*Grainger.*
　Study. Free work.
Cracovienne Fantastique—*Paderewski.*
　Spirited, brilliant, tricky.
Cradle Song—*Brahms.*
　Fundamentals.
* "Crooked Man, The"—*Reimhold* (Brownies) in "Music
　for the Child World."
　Nursery Rhyme. Fantastic.
"Curious Story"—*St. Heller.*
　"My Shadow."
Czardas from "Coppelia"—*Delibes.*
Dance of the Hours—from "Gioconda" *Ponchinelli.*
Dance of the Serpents—*Boccalari.*
　Contrasting moods and movement.
* Dance of the Sprites—*Driscoll.*
　Free work. "Raggedy Ann."
Dans les Bois—*Paganini.*
"Death and the Maiden"—*Schubert.*
Deep River (Negro Spiritual) arr. by *A. W. Kramer.*
　Fundamentals.
Dragon Fly, The—*Nevin.*
　Dainty, sparkling.
Dream Gate—*Bertha Ochsner.* Pub. Burchard Music Co.
　Boston.
　Dance-drama.

* Dream Visions—*Stix*.
> Good to use with balloons and scarfs, has many possibilities.
> "Dance of the Princess and her Companions" in "The Sleeping Princess."
> Waltz time, excellent rhythm and contrasting moods.

* Ecossaisen (excerpt)—*Beethoven*.
> Good 2-4 study.
> Free work.
> Active and happy.

"Elfin Dance"—*Jensen*.

Etude—Op. 75, No. 4—*Schytte*.

Evening Star—from "Tannhauser"—*Wagner*.
> Fundamentals.
> Finale of "The Toilers."

* Fanfare from "Il Trovatore"—*Verdi*.
> Study.
> Joyous, Exhilarating.

Fantasy Piece—Op. 26—*Schumann*.
> Study.

Faust Ballet Waltz—*Gounod*.
> Vigorous.

Faust Waltz—*Gounod*. Vol. II.
> Good waltz with strong accent.

Fifth Nocturne—*Leybach*. Vol. II.
> Fundamentals.

First and Second Waltz in "Dance Album"—*Jensen*.

Five Poems after "Omar Khayyam"—*Arthur Foote*.
> Founded upon "In a Persian Garden."
> Each piece follows the mood of the stanza preceding.

"Flatterer, The"—*Chaminade*. Vol. II.

Fourth Nocturne—*Grieg*.

Funeral March of a Marionette—*Gounod*.
> Used for foot-work.
> Free Work.
> Dance Grotesque.
> "Raggedy Ann and Andy."

Gavotte from "Mignon"—*Thomas*.
    "Pas de Trois."
Gavotte in D—*Gossec*.
General Bum-bum—*Poldini*.
    Free; merry.
* German Dances—*Beethoven*.
    Study.
    Good contrasting moods.
* "Goosey-goosey Gander"—*L. E. Orth*.
    Nursery Rhyme.
Grillen—*Schumann*.
    Whimsical, full of abrupt contrast.
Harlequin Serenade—*Drigo*.
    Fanciful; romantic.
* "Humpty Dumpty"—*Ochsner*.
    Nursery Rhyme.
Hymn to the Sun—"Le Coq d'Or"—*Rimsky-Korsakow*.
    Fundamentals.
    Interpretation.
Idilio—*Lack*.
    Good for work with balloons and scarfs.
Idyll—*Koschat*.
    Waltz—carefree.
Indian Lament—*Dvorak*.
    Fundamentals.
    "The Tapestry."
In My Neighbor's Garden—*Nevin*.
    Bright, tender and sparkling.
Intermezzo—Introduction to Act III from "Jewels of the
    Madonna."—*Wolf—Ferrari*.
    Brilliant Waltz—Varying moods and tempo.
    Good contrasts.
Invitation to the Dance— *Weber*.
    Used for fast foot work.
    Spirited, gay, bright. Rapid tempo.
Irish Tunes from County Derry—*Grainger*.
    Fundamentals.
Isoline Ballet.—(Valse)—*Messager*.

* "Jack-in-the-box"—*Baumselder*—in "Music for the Child World."
"Juggler, The"—*Moszkowski*.
    Character Dance simpler than the one following.
"Juggler, The"—*Moszkowski*.
    Character Dance.
Kammenoi-Ostrow—*Rubenstein*.
    Fundamentals.
"Chorus of Mourners" from "Orpheus and Eurydice."
La Czarine—*Canne*. Vol. II.
    Good Mazurka.
La Migonne—*DeKoven*.
    Study.
Largo—*Handel*. Vol. II.
    Good processional.
Last Greeting, The—*Schubert*.
    "Refugees."
L'Esprit Francaise—*Waldteufel*.
    Playful.
    "Polka for two."
Liebestraum—*Liszt*. Vol. II.
Little Hunters, The—*Kullak*.
    Merry; gay.
*"Little Miss Muffet"—*E. R. Fogg*.
    Nursery Rhyme.
Lorraine March—*Ganne*.
    "Apollo's Chariot."
    Spirited, vigorous.
Love's Dream after the Ball—*Czibulka*. Vol. II.
    Good waltz.
    Smooth flowing rhythm.
Lucia Sextette—*Donizetti*.
    Fundamentals.
March (excerpt)—*Bach*.
    Study.
March from Nut-cracker Suite (excerpt)—*Tschaikowsky*.
    Study.

March from Opus 27 No. 3—*Schubert.*
   Study.
March from "The Christmas Tree"—*Gade.*
   Study.
March from Opus 40 No. 5—*Schubert.*
   Study.
March Herioque—Opus 40 No. 2—*Schubert.*
   Study.
March in D flat—*Hollaender.*
   Study.
   Phrasing.
Marche Militaire—*Schubert.*
   "Greek Games."
Marche Pontificale—*Gounod.*
   Good study for phrasing.
   Pompous and strong.
* "Mary Quite Contrary"—*L. E. Orth.*
   Nursery Rhyme.
* "May Day Gallop"—arranged.
   Study in 2/4 time.
   Circle Dance.
   Many possibilities.
Mazurka from "Coppelia"—*Delibes.*
   Hilarious, gay.
Minuet from "Don Juan"—*Mozart.* Vol. II.
Minuet in G—*Beethoven.*
Minuet—*Paderewski.* Vol. II.
Moment Musicale—*Schubert.* Vol. II.
Moon Moths—*Kissner.*
   Album of three selections.
   Schottische. I.
   Fundamentals—II. and III.
Morning—*Grieg.*
"Natoma Dagger Dance" from "Natoma"—*Herbert*—
   arranged.
"New Doll, The"—*Tschaikowsky.*
   Dance depicting child's delight in her new doll.

* "Old King Cole"—*B. Ochsner.*
  Nursery Rhyme.
"Old Refrain, The"—*Kreisler.*
  Fundamentals.
On the Lake—*Williams.*
  * Elevation—(Excerpt).
On the Wings of Song—*Mendelssohn.*
  Fundamentals.
Orpheus in Hades—*Offenbach*—Part I.
  Used for—"On Mount Parnassus" in "Orpheus and
  Eurydice."
Palms, The—*Faure.*
  Fundamentals.
  Flowing 6/8 time.
Parting March from "Leonore" (excerpt)—*Raff.*
Peer Gynt Suite—*Grieg.*
  Morning.
  Asa's Death.
  Anitra's Dance.
  In the Hall of the Mountain King.
Pirouette—*Finck.*
  Capricious, light, dainty.
Poet and Peasant Overture—*v. Suppe.*
  Used in "Cycle of the Hours."
Polish Dance—*Scharwenka.*
  Vigorous mazurka.
Polonaise Militaire—*Chopin.*
Priests March—*Mendelssohn.*
  Used for "Entrance and Recessional" in "Greek
  Games."
* "Queen of Hearts"—*L. Lehman.*
  Nursery Rhyme.
"Rendezvous, The" *Aletter.*
  Gavotte. Romantic; charming.
Rigadon de Dardanus—*Rameau.*
  Good Study.
Rondino (On a theme by Beethoven)—*Kreisler.*
  Careless and free.

Rosamunde—*Schubert.*
    Free work.
    * "Pan and the Hamadryads"—arranged.
Salto Mortale—*Gurlitt.*
    Free work.
    Playful, tricky.
Scherzo—*Schubert.*
"Schmetterling"—*Merkel.*
    Fundamentals.
Schön Rosmarin—*Kreisler.*
    Light, graceful, gentle, gay.
Second Movement—"Unfinished Symphony"—*Schubert.*
Secret, The—*Gautier.* Vol. II.
    Light and merry.
    "Run, run, run."
Serenade—*Schubert.* Vol. II.
    Fundamentals.
Sextette from "Lucia de Lamermoor." Vol. II.
"Shadow Dance"—*MacDowell.*
Shepherds All and Maidens Fair—*Nevin.*
    Study for 4/4 time.
Shepherds Hey—*Grainger.*
    Free work.
* "Sing a Song of Six-Pence"—*B. Ochsner.*
    Nursery Rhyme.
"Skaters Waltz"—*Waldteufel.*
* "Slave Problem"—Arranged.
    No. 1. *Mendelssohn.*
    No. 2. *Tschaikowsky.*
Slumber Song—*Schumann.*
    Fundamentals.
    Good 6/8 study.
"Soldiers March"—*Schumann.*
Soldiers March from "Faust" (excerpt)—*Gounod.*
    Foot work.
Songs My Mother Taught Me.—*Dvorak.*
    Fundamentals.

Song of the Bargemen on the Volga—arranged by *Aldrich*.
   Fundamentals.
   "The Toilers."
   "The Volga."
Sorrentina—*Lack*.
   Vigorous and exhilarating.
Sous Bois—*Staub*.
   Light, melodious.
Souvenir—*Drdla*. Vol. II.
   Tender, melodious.
Special Rhythmic Studies.
    1. *Beethoven*—opus 28 (excerpt).
    2. * Elevation.
    3. * Free 6/8 rhythm.
    4. * *Greig*—The Brooklet (excerpt).
    5. * Rhythms for sliding.
    6. 6/8 rhythm for foot work.
    7. "Studies"—*Demarest*.
    8. * Study—4/4 (slow).
    9. * Study—4/4 (strong, lively).
   10. * Studies for leaping—different tempos.
   11. * Study—*Salisbury*.
   12. * *Schubert*—2/4, and 3/4.
   13. * Waltz for balancing—3/4.
   14. "Study 3/4 run."
Spring Zephyrs—*Vessela*.
   Exhilarating, breezy.
Storm, The—"William Tell"—*Rossini*.
Stradella Overture—*Flowtow*.
   "Dance of the Maenads" in "Orpheus and Eurydice."
   Frenzied.
"Swan, The"—*Saint Saens*. Vol. II.
Swedish Wedding March—No. 1. *Soderman*.
   Free Work.
Swiss Maid.
   Merry.
Symphony No. 6 (Pathetique) *Tschaikowsky*—1st Mov.
   Finale in "Sleeping Princess."

Tanzweise—*Meyer-Helmund.*
    Good Polka.
    "The Milkmaid."
    "The Pool."
* "The Toad's Mistake"—*Bentley and Loomis*—"Play Songs."
    Nursery Rhyme.
To a Wild Rose—*MacDowell.*
    "Instrumentation of the Dance."
Torch Light Dance—*Meyerbeer.*
    Good Study.
Traumerei—*Schumann.* Vol. II.
    Thoughtful; dreamy.
Turkish March from "The Ruins of Athens"—*Beethoven.*
    Free work.
    Vivacious.
Valse Bleue—*Margis.* Vol. II.
Valse Lente—from Coppelia—*Delibes.*
Valse Lente—*Schuett*—Op. A 17 No. 2.
Valse Lente—from "Sylvia"—*Delibes.*
Valse Triste—*Sibelius.*
    "The Fairy Thorn." "Arachne."
Voices of Spring—*Strauss.*
    "Ballet d'Action."
    Joyous, exhilarating waltz.
Wah-wah-taysee—*Cadman.*
    Study.
    Light, Crisp.
Waltz Collections.
    Brahms—Opus 39 (Nos. 8 and 15); Vol. VIII.
    Chopin—Opus 18.
    Schubert—Waltzes.
Waltz in E—*Moszkowski.*
Warrior Song—*Heller.*
    "Pyrrhic Dance."
Wedding Day at Troldhaugen—*Greig.*
    "The Moonbeams and the Sunbeam."
"Whirlwind, The"—*Krantz.*

Why—*Schumann*—Vol. VIII.
    Fundamentals.
    Study.
Wild Horseman—*Schumann*.
    Free Work.
    Excellent rhythmic study.
William Tell Overture—*Rossini*.
    1. Dawn.
    2. Storm.
    "Dance of Leaves and Wind" in "Ceres and Persephone."
    3. Calm.
With Castanets—*Reinecke*.
    "The Little Vagabond."
Woodland Echoes—*MacDowell*.

Albums

Beethoven—Sonatas.
Bentley, Alys E.—"Play Songs."
Chopin—Waltzes.
German, Edw.—Three Dances.
Gounod—Ballet Music.
    Mirror Dance No. 6.—"The Little Vagabond."
Nubian Slaves No. 1—Good Waltz.
Grieg.—The Theo. Presser Publication.
    Peer Gynt Suite.
Hofer, Mari—Music for the Child World—Vol. II.
Kullak, Opus 62—Scenes from Childhood.
MacDowell, Edward—Woodland Sketches.
Piano Pieces the Whole World Plays—Vols. II and VIII.
Schubert—Dances.
Schumann—Album for the Young, Opus 68.
Schytte—Opus 58.
    Opus 75 "Chord Grasps."
Tschaikowsky—Album for the Young—Opus 39.

Appendix: Plan of Lessons

A Suggested Plan of Twenty-Four Lessons for Beginners.
(College Age)

It will be readily appreciated that any series of lessons can only propose a plan—as the rapidity in progress will be affected by many conditions, such as age and previous training of the class, and skill of the teacher.

The aim in any scheme of lessons at first and for some time should be general, stimulating interest, and giving a variety of experiences.

Length of period should be at least forty minutes, preferably sixty minutes. (This plan is built on a sixty minute basis).

Class should meet at least once a week—preferably oftener.

Suitable costumes should be required; such as will permit of entire freedom of movement, and with some claim to the artistic.

Lesson I

1. Explain costume.
2. Give discussion about the work and its method of approach. Aim to get an intellectual attitude and to stimulate interest.

Lesson II

1. First Roll—Plate VIII, page 247.
   See IV-2-A page 131.
   Music: *Schubert's* Serenade.

2. Flexion and extension of spine 1-A page 64.
Aim for "follow-thru" of movement. Explain.
Music: Song of the Bargemen.
3. Discuss the different types of locomotion; i. e. the elemental activities.
4. Explain note values.
5. Take note values with the corresponding elemental activities. For whole, half, quarter, and eighth notes have pianist play chords—for dotted eighth and sixteenth notes use * "Galop."
6. Repeat using a good march—Hollaender's March in D flat.
7. Phrasing:
Music: * May Day Galop.
8. Explain Pitch.
9. Carry all over into * "Fanfare."

Lesson III

1. Spine work continued.
2. Movements of the shoulder girdle and arms. See page 73.
3. Carry over into First Roll.
Music: Irish Tune from County Derry.
4. "Metrical Accentuation." Page 156.
Use various ways of bringing out the beat. Distinguish between 2/4 (May Day Galop), 3/4 (* Schubert Waltz), 4/4 (Shepherds All and Maidens Fair), and 6/8 (Slumber Song—*Schumann*) time.
5. "Rhythmical Accentuation." Page 158.
6. "Crescendo" and "dimuendo" of movement.
Music: Ecossaissen.

"Staccato" music: Gavotte in D; "Legato" music: Andante Op. 13 *Beethoven*.

7. Carry 4, 5, and 6 over into Circle Skip.
Music: May Day Galop.

Lesson IV

1. Back, shoulder and arm work continued.
2. Carry over into further development of first roll.
Music: Schmetterling.
3. Leg work. Refer to II page 90.
4. Musical appreciation and rhythm ad lib.
5. "Adaptive response"—whole class working together in twos. Music: Swedish Wedding March.

Lesson V

1. Fundamentals ad lib.
2. Continue leg work.
3. Coördinate legs and back. III page 117.
4. Incorporate all knowledge to this point in dance forms.
(a) Large circles—May Day Galop.
(b) In threes—Skip for Three.
(c) In twos—Ecossaissen.
(d) Whole class in threes—Shepherds Hey.
5. "The Bacchanale"—music arranged.

Lesson VI

1. Fundamentals ad lib.
Music: See list.
(Advancement depends on improvement in motor control).

2. Consideration of foot work and different bases—carried over into problems with dramatic content.
   a. When driven on by fear.
   b. Creeping along quietly with idea of surprising someone.
   c. When weary and depressed.
   d. When carrying a heavy load.
   e. Old age.
   f. Peacock Strut.
      Heels are raised off the floor, base is ball of feet.
      Weight is transferred from ball to toes—knees bent.
      Head arches proudly. Is slight flexion from side to side.
   g. Contrasting moods.
   h. A good free easy walk.
      Music: a, b, c, d, e—Chord Grasps—*Schytte*.
             f. —Opus 58 No. 3—*Schytte*.
             g. * Studies—*Demarest*.
             h. Any good march.
3. * "Fanfare."

Lesson VII

1. Fundamentals ad lib. with special reference to upper back and arm control preparatory for the Second Roll.
2. Special study of a piece of music for dancing.
   Music: * Schubert Study.
3. Dancing "at sight."
   Music: Grieg Study; Elfin Dance *Jensen*.
4. "Polka for Two."
   Music: L'Esprit Francaise.

Lesson VIII

1. Fundamentals ad lib.
2. Second Roll. Plate IX, page 248.   See also page 135.
3. Further work on legs and feet.
4. Carry over "reaching" from hip in waltz movement forward and backward.
   Music: Valse Bleue.
5. Work out the First Roll in the upright position.
6. Turn with different leads.
   Music: Schmetterling.
7. Carry over into waltzing using the arms in various combinations.
8. "Slide and hop" with attention to form.
   Music: Sorrentina.
9. "The Bacchanale."

Lesson IX

1. Fundamentals ad lib.
2. First Roll with good control.
3. Second Roll.
4. Combinations of arm work with the different elemental activities.
   Music: 2/4, 4/4, 3/4, 6/8 time.
5 Further study as to building phrases with sequences of steps.
   Music: L'Esprit Francaise.
6. "Polka for Two."
   Music: L'Esprit Francaise.

Lesson X

1. Unfolding and Folding.
2. First Roll.
3. Second Roll.
4. Coördinate back, head and arms.
5. Walking.
6. Walking with changes in positions of back, head and arms.
7. Carry 4 over into the development of a frieze.
   Music: Adagietto—Dance out with "Fanfare."
8. "Polka for Two."
   Music: L'Esprit Francaise.

Lesson XI

1. Folding and Unfolding.
2. Second Roll.
3. Leaping, skipping, running, etc., with dramatic content.
   Music: * Studies—Demarest.
4. "Hop-step-draw" with strong movements.
   Music: "Wild Horseman"—*Schumann*.
5. * Study—*Salisbury*.
6. "The Bacchanale."

Lesson XII

1. Continue study of fundamentals and dance composition, working for excellency of technique.
2. Use balloons with high leaping and hopping.
3. Combine high skipping—"slide-hop" with rapid whirl— then a sudden strong lunge forward—hold to end of phrase. Repeat.

Music: Faust Waltz.

4. Backward turning with a lunge forward at completion of turn.
   Music: Schmetterling.
5. Dance with balloon.
   Music. Idilio.
6. "Adaptive response" in groups of threes.
   Music: *Chopin* Prelude No. 7.

Lesson XIII

1. Same as XII-1.
2. Leaping and hopping in form.
   Music: Sorrentina.
3. Combine turns with leaping.
   Music: Faust Waltz.
4. Turns with different leads. Explain law of opposition.
   Move in different directions; arms in different planes, hands clasped in different positions.
   Work with strong and gentle movements. Get good contrast.
5. Review "The Bacchanale."

Lesson XIV

1. Fundamentals continued with special reference to control of back and shoulder girdle in second roll.
2. Fundamentals with special reference to legs and back.
3. Dance with scarfs.
4. Group dance with scarf.
   Music: * *Schubert* Waltzes.

Lesson XV

1. Fundamentals with special reference to the Crawl.
2. Review principles of dance composition.
3. " Old King Cole."
   Music: * Old King Cole.

Lesson XVI

1. Folding and Unfolding.
2. Frieze—Music: Adagietto.
   Dance out with *Moszkowski* Waltz in E.
3. Free work with balloons.
4. Dance: Two Girls with a Balloon.
   Music: "Dream Visions."

Lesson XVII

1. Folding and Unfolding—first and second roll ad lib.
2. Further development of the crawl.
3. Large, vigorous movements with scarfs.
4. Dancing "at sight." (Improvisation.)
   See bibliography of Music.
5. Any of the previous dances and studies ad lib.

Lessons XVIII to XXIV

Preceding work ad lib.

The progression in the remaining lessons should be in control and skill in execution with special reference to the ROLLS, FOLDING and UNFOLDING, and the CRAWL.

Advancement in expression comes with improved motor control and growth in imagination and emotional capacity.

An examination should be given at the close of the term. including (see suggested classifications, pages 51–52).

1. Fundamentals—to test conscious muscular control.
2. Rhythm—to test the understanding of the working materials out of which the dance is constructed.
3. Impromptu dancing for quickness and accuracy in response to various rhythms and spontaneity and spirit.
4. An original dance.

Through portals of the Spring we come again
To offer you our wordless poetry.
All that we sing of splendor and of joy,
All that we sing that sounds the note of fears,
We give because our souls, as yours, are wrought
Of sighs and songs and dreams, deep laughter, too.

The Dance

As Interpreted by Pupils

========of========

Margaret N. H'Doubler

May 29, 1924   Open Air Theatre

University of Wisconsin

PART I.

1. Frieze--*Bizet; Brahms*
2. Nocturne----------------------------------*Chopin, Opus 9, No. 2*
3. Run, run, run--*Gautier*
4. Mazurka--- *Blumenschein*
5. Idyllio--*Lack*
6. Arachne---*Sibelius*

> *Whom the gods a spider turned, to weave eternally*
> *This hour your frail, curved arms be free! And joyous see*
> *The glory in the wind and sun and 'ere the hour be done*
> *Make this freedom an endless dream of supreme ecstasy.*

7. The Volga-------------------------------*Russian Folk Song*

> *By the deep—flowing river—The Volga*
> *The slow wrack, the slow pain, the beautified toil,*
> *The wrenching of souls as they lost them and found them,*
> *By the deep—flowing river—The Volga.*

8. Serenata--*Moszkowski*
9. Bacchanale--*Arranged*

> *Yours is the glad dance, breathless enrapture!*
> *Yours is the mad dance, as quivering you capture*
> *Full-throated the Circean wine, bewitching*
> *Your body and spirit. For a moment enriching*
> *The beauty of being!*

10. Tarentella--*Rubenstein*

> *To the life of her, to the death of her*
> *Dance ye maids!*
> *For the wound is deeply bit. Exuberant*
> *Be the joy, the gleam in your eyes*
> *That to death ye danced with her.*

11. Rendezvous---*Aletter*

> *Musing 'mong the statues, the old gardener of Versailles sleeps.*
> *Sweep then the white lovers from their ped'stals to their long waited*
> *   trysting.*
> *Sweet the embrace of their spirits in dance, and wistful.*
> *Stirs then the gardener. Quiet shadows—But the rose?*

12. Scarfs---*Gounod*

PART II.

PETITES ETUDES

1. Jolly Peter——————————————————*Werner-Kerstein*

   A puckery smile and twinkling feet
   You're tatters of sunlight, Jolly Pete!

2. Little Miss Muffet—————————————————*Arranged*

   Little Miss Muffett had a provoking tuffet,
   Which had been brought up in the wrong way.
   She had a spider, who'd always chide her
   As she munched her curds and whey.
   She sat on the tuffet, her mouth she stuffed it
   Much to the tuffet's dismay.
   Then up danced the spider and openly defied her,
   Which comes of curds, stowed away.

3. Raggedy Ann and Andy—————————————*Gounod*

4. I am the Cat————————————————————*Demarest*

   I was the cat who walked alone
   And to whom all things were the same
   'Till glorified jazz my tail defamed
   And now I must live to atone.

5. Captain Bing was a Pirate King————*Father Goose Rhyme*

6. Visions——————————————————————*Schumann*

   Moon's over the sky's edge and I would go!
   But my way leads on the star's tips, where they reflected glow;
   Yet all those tiny points were made and scattered so
   That the silver moon seems just beyond and its touch
      I'll never know.

7. An Harlequinade——————————————————*Ghys*

PART III.

"THE FANTASTIQUE"

Music written and played by———————*Charles Demarest*

The petulant and petted Child Infanta
Gives orders that a court in miniature
Be held to honor her ten childish years.
She enters in a manner frankly bored
And views herself, well pleased, within the glass.
Betimes a juggler, quick of trick, performs,
And after him, two gypsies are announced
They glide about and tell strange tales of Fate.
They dance! They whirl! They spin away again.
Then comes the great surprise—a little dwarf!
He quite delights the Princess, and she throws
A rose to him, as she and all the children
Trip away to taste the birthday feast.
The little half-wild human thing stays on
Exulting o'er his fragrant precious rose.
But then he finds a cruel companion
In the glass, and finding it he learns—
The truth—It is himself!
Truth breaks his crippled heart, and with its breaking
Death comes to soothe his crooked, crippled life.

DRAMATIS PERSONAE

Edith Boys
Mona Brown
Margaret Callsen
Janet Cumming
Reinette Douglas
Esther Fowler
Maurine Hall
Blanche Hayes
Caroline Hinsdell
Josephine Jung
Doris Lingenfelder
Elaine Mabley
Margaret Murray

Elna Mygdal
Bertha Ochsner
Ida Rappaport
Edna Rasmusen
Catherine Rice
Helen Robinson
Esther Rosenberg
Lucille Salentine
Elizabeth Sehon
Eleanor Sikes
Dorothy Simpson
Dorothy Sutor
Doris Taylor
Rhea Whale

Music: Piano —Mary A. Trumpf, Charles Demarest
Violins—Ruth Perssion, Sylvia Rosenberg
Cello —John Bach

Student Chairman--Helen Robinson
Costumes-------------------------------------Lee Bacon and Beatrice Marx
Lines------------------------------Catherine Davis and Reinette Douglas
Assistant Director--Janet Cumming
General Director------------------------------------Margaret N. H'Doubler
Mirror designed by Catherine Rice.

See next two pages for
STUDENTS' PROGRESS CARD

I. Fundamental Motor Control.
> Note general flexibility and coördination of movement. Is there continuity of movement? If not, where is movement restricted? Is proper balance maintained? Is correct base taken?

A. Rolls.
1. First roll.
   a. Head.
   b. Shoulders.
   c. Arms.
   d. Legs.
   e. Hands.
   f. Change of lead.
2. Second Roll.
   a. Head.
   b. Shoulders.
   c. Arms.
   d. Hands.
   e. Lower back and abdominal control.
   f. Legs.
   g. Change of lead.
3. Third roll.
   a. Head.
   b. Shoulder.
   c. Arms.
   d. Lower back and abdominal control.
   e. Legs.
   f. Change of lead.

B. Folding and unfolding.
1. Balance.
2. Head.
3. Shoulders.
4. Arms.
5. Localized control of spine.
6. Lower back and abdominal control.
7. Change of lead.
8. Feet.

C. Crawl.
1. Head.
2. Shoulder.
3. Arms.
4. Hands.
5. Spine—Localized control and change of lead.
6. Legs.

D. Posture.

PROGRESS CARD [1]

II. Realization and Appreciation of Music through Movement.
  A. Elementary steps.
    1. Walking —forward —backward —sideward—turning and taken in all possible directions and combinations.
    2. Running........Same.
    3. Leaping.........Same.
    4. Hopping........Same.
    5. Skipping ....Same.
    6. Galloping.......Same.
    7. Sliding..........Same.
    8. Combinations of elementary steps.
        a. Waltz.   c. Polka.
        b. Two-step.   d. Schottische.
                           e. Original combinations.
  B. Phrasing.
    1. Expressed by
        a. Change of direction.   f. Localizing the response
        b. Change of accent.   in different parts of the
        c. Change of intensity.   body.
        d. Change of step.   g. Accurate discrimina-
        e. Association of ideas,   tion of the kinæsthetic
           imagination and fancy.   sense (without music).
    2. All carried over into the analysis of some selection of music.

III. The dance.—All of I and II carried over into dance construction.
    1. Class problems.
    2. Improvisation.
    3. Original dances.

[1] Use both sides of card if necessary.